A gift for

_____

from

_____

A Certain Je Ne Sais Quoi

Words We Pinched From Other Languages

'They have been at a great feast of languages, and stolen the scraps.'

William Shakespeare, *Love's Labour's Lost*, V.i

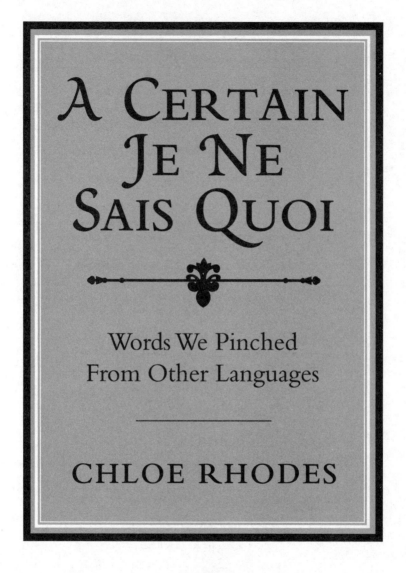

A Certain Je Ne Sais Quoi

Words We Pinched From Other Languages

CHLOE RHODES

Michael O'Mara Books Limited

First published in Great Britain in 2009 by
Michael O'Mara Books Limited
9 Lion Yard
Tremadoc Road
London SW4 7NQ

A CIP catalogue record for this book is available from the British Library.

Papers used by Michael O'Mara Books Limited are natural,
recyclable products made from wood grown in sustainable forests.
The manufacturing processes conform to the environmental
regulations of the country of origin.

ISBN: 978-1-84317-364-9

1 2 3 4 5 6 7 8 9 10

www.mombooks.com

Cover design by Ana Bjezancevic

Design and typesetting by Ed Pickford

Illustrations by Andrew Pinder

Printed and bound in Great Britain by Clays Ltd, St Ives plc

Introduction

The wonderful thing about words is that once we've learnt their meanings, we rarely have to give them a second thought. Whether we're arguing a point, expressing our passion or simply ordering a pizza, the words are there; generally we have no need to pause to consider their precise meanings or ponder over their provenance.

However, for all the benefits such fluency brings, it does mean that we're often oblivious to the fascinating origins of the words and phrases we use every day, which is why this book came to be. The list of words and phrases within it is by no means exhaustive, and it doesn't offer an academic look at etymology, but it does attempt to tell the stories of some of the thousands of foreign words and phrases that have come to be commonly used in English.

That there are so many should come as no surprise; English speakers have been linguistic magpies since at least the fifth century, when the dialects of Anglo-Saxon settlers, Celts and Norse invaders were cobbled together to create Old English. When the Normans arrived in 1066 it must have seemed only natural to appropriate some of their vocabulary too; by the end of the thirteenth century, more than 10,000 French words had been absorbed into English, 75 per cent of which we continue to use today. The Norman conquerors also shared with us a fondness for Latin, both Ancient Gaul and Britain having been invaded by the Romans in 58 BC and AD 43 respectively, and a few centuries later the European Renaissance brought Latin and Ancient Greek to the fore once more.

As the British Empire grew from the late sixteenth to the early twentieth centuries, our marauding, seafaring forebears filled their boats not only with strange Asian spices and exotic fabrics, but words for all the new foods, animals and items of clothing they'd seen. In North America, meanwhile, English was to receive its most vigorous boost yet. Words from Italy, Spain (via Mexico), Poland, Germany and Eastern Europe were soon spilling from the immigrant ships to be mopped up by the giant lexical sponge of American English.

Very often the new terms had no practical purpose – English speakers didn't go around gobbling up foreign words because they were short of their own – they did it because, where self-expression is concerned, you can never have too many options. Very often there is just something about throwing in a foreign word or phrase that lends whatever we have to say, well – how best to put it? – a certain *je ne sais quoi*.

A Note from the Publisher:

The convention in written English is to place unfamiliar foreign terms, or relatively newly acquired ones, in italics. Opinions differ as to when a word has been so fully absorbed into English that it no longer needs italics, but our vade mecums (see p.167) have been the eminently reliable *New Oxford Dictionary for Writers and Editors* and the *New Oxford Spelling Dictionary*.

Acknowledgements

Thanks to Matt Hibberd, John Rhodes, Cassie Kite, Kerry Chapple and Lindsay Davies. Thanks also to Dan Crompton, Lirios Pla-Miro, Sarah Rustin, Jenny Fry, Jamie Buchan, Rowena Anketell and all the linguists at Michael O'Mara for their generous help.

A cappella

in the manner of the chapel or choir
(Italian, from the Latin *'a cappella'*)

This phrase comes to us via the Late Latin *'cappa'*, meaning 'cap' or 'cloak' – the chapel which housed the cloak of St Martin, kept as a relic, was thus the *'capella'*. The meaning of the term has now expanded to include any unaccompanied vocal performance, from the do-wop bands of 1950s America to Barbershop quartets to modern TV talent shows.

The neighbourhood dogs all howled along when Jeremy began his a cappella *serenade.*

À la carte

according to the menu (French)

An 'à la carte' menu features individually priced items as opposed to a set price menu. The concept was introduced by celebrated French chef Georges Auguste Escoffier during his tenure at the Carlton Hotel in London at the turn of the last century. Escoffier's 1903 cookbook *Le Guide culinaire* is still revered as a culinary bible, though his greatest claim to fame is that one of his pupils was Ho Chi Minh, who presumably thought he'd better get a bit of pastry practice under his belt before leading Vietnam to independence.

'It'll have to be the à la carte menu for me; I've got a terrible craving for truffles.'

À la mode
fashionable (French)

The link between France and fashion was established by King Louis XIV, whose court became such an epicentre of good taste that the British aristocracy didn't simply want to dress in French fashion, they wanted their phrase for it too. In the seventeenth century the term was anglicized to become 'alamode' – a light silk used to make scarves. In the US the phrase has also come to mean 'with ice-cream'; there must have been a time in small town America when the combined flavours of cooked apple, sweet pastry and vanilla represented the very latest in fashionable, cutting-edge gastronomy.

'Can I suggest these divine little ankle boots, madam? Python-skin platforms are so à la mode.'

A priori
from what precedes (Latin)

In philosophical debate, 'a priori' knowledge is a form of knowledge that comes from what we know rationally to be true, without having to test or research it. Its opposite is 'a posteriori' knowledge, which is gleaned through experimentation or experience. The great eighteenth-century German philosopher Immanuel Kant initiated the modern use of the term and believed that a priori knowledge was transcendental, stemming from an individual's cognitive faculties. In more general terms it is used literally or ironically for any argument or idea that is based on inherent knowledge rather than observation.

'We know a priori that Tom won't say no to some kind of dinner; it doesn't matter what we get, that boy will eat anything.'

Ad hoc

for this (Latin)

This is one of many politically, administratively and commercially useful terms to have retained its Latin form. It means something that is designed for one set purpose. 'Ad hoc' committees are established by the government to help solve a specific problem; they're usually created in response to an urgent need and last only for the duration of the task in hand. This has led the phrase to have a broader meaning of improvised or provisional. For example, if plans are said to be 'ad hoc' they might be seen as last-minute and haphazard.

Jeffrey preferred to plan his plane-spotting trips for himself; the itineraries of his fellow enthusiast seemed alarmingly ad hoc.

Ad lib

according to one's pleasure (Latin, from '*ad libitum*')

This was originally used to mark out the points within a piece of sheet music or theatrical script where performers could add their own personal flourish. In modern times the phrase is most often used to describe the unscripted, off-the-cuff comments that comedians, actors or presenters add to their scripted material, either to get an extra laugh or to conceal the fact that they have forgotten their lines.

> *'Oh, darlings, that was awful! The words just went right out of my head, I had to ad lib my way through the death scene.'*

Ad nauseam

to sickness (Latin)

An *'argumentum ad nauseam'* is an argument that is repeated until everyone is sick of hearing it. Much of the language of debate comes from the adversarial conventions established by Roman orator Cicero in the first century BC. 'Ad nauseam' has been used in English since the early 1600s and is still employed to pour scorn on a well-rehearsed political argument. It's also used in reference to other annoyingly repetitive things, like people who recite lines from their favourite TV comedy until you want to tear your ears off.

> *'Late again, Stevenson; don't try to explain, I've heard your excuses ad nauseam.'*

⋙◦⋘

Aficionado

ardent fan or devotee (Spanish)

In Spain 'aficionado' is used most frequently to describe fans of bullfighting. Ernest Hemingway was a famous one; '*Aficion* means passion,' says his narrator Jake Barnes in *The Sun Also Rises*. In English the term indicates a devoted fan of a sport or art form that evokes strong, primal feelings. There are jazz, opera, rugby and ballet aficionados, but you're unlikely to hear the term applied to badminton fans, no matter how potent their ardour for the perfect drop-volley.

Sid 'The Savage' Simmons lived in fear of being outed as a figure-skating aficionado; he'd been smitten since he saw Torville and Dean dance to Ravel's Boléro.

⋙◦⋘

Agent provocateur

inciting agent (French)

A secret agent employed by the police or government to encourage criminals or dissidents to break the law so that they can be arrested. The phrase is still used in this way; in the US, the FBI has used agents provocateurs to infiltrate radical political groups like the Black Panthers and the Ku Klux Klan, and in the UK it's the name of a risqué lingerie firm that hopes to incite bad behaviour of a different kind – *ooh la la!*

> *'Agent Peters, we need you in there as an agent provocateur. Your undercover name will be "The Strangler."'*

Agitprop

agitation and propaganda (Russian,
from '*agitatsii i propagandy*')

The Agitation and Propaganda section of the Communist Party's Central Committee was responsible for the education of the people after the 1917 Revolution. It used speeches, radio broadcasts, posters, film and visual art to influence public opinion, though in Soviet Russia at that time there was no negative connotation to the word 'propaganda'. In modern Western usage it usually refers to political propaganda, especially of dissident or protesting groups, but also works of art and literature whose aim is to indoctrinate its audience with extreme leftist ideology.

Frederick feigned illness on the night of the Socialist Amateur Dramatic Society's monthly wine and poetry evening. He'd had his fill of agitprop at the last one.

Aide-memoire

memory aid (French)

Early use of the phrase, which means a note or memorandum, was limited to military and diplomatic fields. G. Lewis's 1846 book *Aide-Mémoire to the Military Sciences* was one of the first written references to it. In more recent times it has also come to refer to a memory-jogging symbol, like a knot tied in a handkerchief, or a mnemonic device, like the rhyme 'i before e except after c'.

Mr Green's scowl was putting off the voters, so his political advisers drew smiley faces on each page of his speech as an aide-memoire to look more cheerful.

Al dente

to the tooth (Italian)

This is the term Italians use to describe the way pasta should be served – cooked through but still firm, retaining some bite. The enormous popularity of Italian food in Britain and the US has led the phrase to be widely used in English. It has also been adopted to describe vegetables like green beans or courgettes, which have been cooked briefly so they retain a bit of crunch.

The craze for al dente vegetables hadn't really caught on at Mrs Higginson's guesthouse: her greens were so well cooked you had to eat them with a spoon.

━━⟨⟩━━

Al fresco

in the fresh (Italian)

In English, we use the phrase to mean 'in the fresh air', but to Italians it's a slang term for 'in prison', like the English phrase 'in the cooler'. To avoid confusion when visiting Italy, ask for a table '*all'aperto*' meaning 'in the open' if you want to dine, erm, al fresco. The phrase has been used in English since at least the eighteenth century – the picnic at Box Hill in Jane Austen's *Emma* is described as an 'al-fresco party'.

'I'd rather not eat al fresco again; last night I lost half my spaghetti to a seagull.'

━━⟨⟩━━

Algebra

reunion, restoration (Latin, from Arabic '*al-jabr*')

Ninth-century Persian mathematician Muhammad bin Musa al-Khawarizmi first used the term to describe the methods by which letters and other symbols are used to represent numbers and quantities in equations and formulae. In fact, the romanized version was first used in English in reference to reuniting broken bones. In the twelfth century a Latin translation of al-Khawarizmi's work was published and we have used 'algebra' as a mathematical term ever since.

Sarah had found a pleasing way to practise the balancing principles of algebra – every time she ate one of her own sweets, she ate one of her brother's too.

Alma mater

nourishing mother (Latin)

Your 'alma mater' is your university or school. The phrase was originally used by the Romans as a title for goddesses, and by early Christians to describe the Virgin Mary. '*Alma mater studorum*', which translates as 'nourishing mother of studies' was the motto of the University of Bologna in Italy – the oldest university in the world – and it may have been through this association that the term came to refer to places of education. Its meaning has extended in the US to mean the school song or anthem.

Boris could barely contain his excitement on the way to the reunion at his alma mater. Ten years had passed since his failed attempt to woo Tiffany Plumbings, and he felt ready to give it another go.

❧

Alter ego

other self (Latin)

The phrase, in the sense of a second self or alternative persona, was first used in reference to schizophrenia in the early nineteenth century. It is now also used to refer to a number of more benign double identities; from cross-dressers to authors whose characters are fictionalized versions of themselves. An alter ego has even become a fashionable accessory in the music business. David Bowie started it with Ziggy Stardust: Britney Spears, Mariah Carey and Beyoncé Knowles each have one, and Prince has two.

Barry in accounts seemed like such a mild-mannered and steady man, and yet the rumour was that he had an alter ego – Rosalita Lamé – and performed at the local cabaret club every other Friday.

---◦◦◦◦---

Amok/amuck, to run

furious attack (Malay)

The word comes from the Malay description of a psychiatric disturbance, in which the sufferer is first subdued or even depressed before suddenly becoming wild, maniacal and usually violent towards others. It is still used to describe the condition of people who commit a sudden, unprovoked attack, but it has also developed a colloquial meaning. When people are said to be 'running amok', like rioters, for example, they are acting wildly and without rational self-control.

Police had to be called to a major department store sale today after shoppers ran amok in the white-goods department.

---◦◦◦◦---

Amuse-bouche

mouth amuser (French)

Something to tickle the taste buds before the arrival of a starter, an '*amuse-bouche*' will never appear on a menu, as it is complimentary and chosen by the chef. The concept of a bite-sized taster of the chef's signature style was introduced as part of the nouvelle cuisine movement, which specializes in offering small, beautifully presented and intensely flavoured courses. In France the colloquial phrase '*amuse-gueule*' ('*gueule*' being slang for mouth) is more often used.

'Tonight, mademoiselle, we have a speciality of roasted sea bass in a tarragon jus and to begin, an amuse-bouche *of green pea and mint sorbet in a crisp parmesan tuile.'*

Angst

fear (German)

Angst is generally translated simply as fear, but is often used to describe a profound horror, or existential dread, as coined by German philosophers in the mid 1800s. English novelist George Eliot wrote of '*Die Angst*', which brought on a pain in the heart and the word became more widespread in English after the translation of Austrian psychologist Sigmund Freud's work. The 1980s saw the birth of teen angst – based on the sense of injustice and futility that comes with raging hormones, and you can now regularly find sports fans and businesspeople 'angsting' over match results and corporate deals.

'I've never known anything to cause as much angst as this week's fixtures list.'

Annus horribilis

horrible year (Latin)

A pun on '*annus mirabilis*', which described a year of British victories in the eighteenth century, this phrase was first used in the Queen's speech at the end of 2002. Her year had been marred by the breakdown of three royal marriages and a devastating fire at Windsor Castle. Two years later, Kofi Annan, then the UN Secretary General, repeated the phrase to describe a year in which the UN's Iraq 'Oil for Food' programme had been tainted by charges of corruption. It is now used widely to describe a bad year.

With the highest rainfall on record this really has been an annus horribilis *for fans of beach volleyball.*

Anorak

heavy hooded jacket (Greenland Inuit)

The cosy, hooded '*anoraq*' is the garment worn by the Inuit peoples of the Arctic to protect them against the very harshest weather conditions. In the 1960s the 'anorak' became popular in Britain as a style of jacket with a fur-trimmed hood beloved of Mods. The European version was a prototype for the technical clothing that evolved later for mountaineers, sailors, cavers and other adventurers. At the time it was innocent of negative associations. Today the word is used pejoratively for an enthusiast interested in information regarded as boring or unfathomable by the rest of us, probably because it's long been favoured by trainspotters.

Rodney, an unashamed enthusiast for technical detail, was wearing a high-quality Gore-Tex anorak on the day he rescued three barely-dressed fashionistas caught in a blizzard.

Appellation contrôlée

officially certified origin (French)

This refers to '*appellation d'origine contrôlée*', the French system of guaranteeing the specific origin of their wines. Established in 1935, this method of classification controls seven aspects of the wine producing process: the land vines are grown on, grape varieties used, viticultural methods (pruning and fertilization), yield, alcohol content, historical practices employed and the taste, which are all tested before certification is given. In Britain and the US our familiarity with the term is generally restricted to reading it on a wine label with a sigh of satisfied anticipation.

'Ah-ha, an Appellation Bordeaux Contrôlée – *perfect with roast beef!'*

Après-ski

after skiing (French)

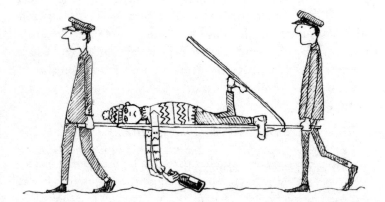

'Après-ski' is used in English to describe the activities, primarily the nightlife, indulged in at ski resorts once the sun goes down. In the Alps the first après-ski drink is usually enjoyed in a bar near to the slopes while you're still sporting your ski wear. In France the term actually refers simply to the snow boots that you change into once you've taken your skis off, but most people would agree that the anglicized version has wider appeal. In the US its meaning is broader still and extends to the general ambience of a resort.

Susan loved her winter breaks though she never actually hit the slopes; she preferred to save her energy for the après-ski.

Apropos

on the subject of (French, from '*à propos de*')

There are several interlinked definitions for this phrase; the first is used, as in French, for 'on the subject of', but more broadly it has come to mean 'pertinent to', or 'apt'. For example: 'an excellent point, and very apropos'. But it can also be used for 'by the way', or 'incidentally', when you're saying something that isn't to the point at all, but seems worth saying anyway.

I should probably point out, apropos, that there are many foreign phrases that we use very liberally in English without ever having the faintest idea what they actually mean.

Arriviste

a person who has arrived (French)

An arriviste is someone who has risen to a higher rank in society but hasn't yet earned the respect of those they're joining. It was first used widely during the dramatic class changes that took place during the Industrial Revolution in Britain, when working-class families were able to ascend the social ladder with money made through enterprise rather than inheritance. In English the phrase is synonymous with 'social climber' and, in a modern context, it might be used to describe someone who is rather thrusting or pushy.

Lady Budley-Hoebottom was determined not to make eye contact with Miss Carter. She was an arriviste if ever there was one – fake tan and acrylic nails always gave the game away.

Ars longa, vita brevis

the art is long, life is short (Latin)

This aphorism was coined by Ancient Greek physician Hippocrates, and comes from a longer quotation, which translates as, 'Life is short, the art [in the sense of craft or skill] long, opportunity fleeting, experiment dangerous, judgement difficult.' Hippocrates had surmised that none of us should be too hard on ourselves if we make mistakes, given that life is generally a very tricky business. In modern use the 'life is short' bit has assumed a greater significance, and is often quoted to remind someone to make the most of every minute (see *Carpe diem*).

'Don't beat yourself up about it, Dave, you'll pass next time – ars longa, vita brevis *and all that.'*

Art nouveau

new art (French)

This was the international style of art and architecture which developed in the late 1800s and took its name from a Parisian gallery called the Maison de l'Art Nouveau, though, ironically, the French themselves often used the English term 'modern style' to describe it. In Britain the architect Charles Rennie Mackintosh (1868–1928) was the movement's leading practitioner. The popularity of the style gave rise to many copies and now we also use the term to describe designs that imitate the art nouveau style.

Veronica's collection of coffee cups was her pride and joy – her favourite was a little pink one that she thought was rather art nouveau.

Assassin

hashish-eater (Arabic, from '*Hashshashin*')

No, I asked for an aspirin.

The Assassins, also known as the Hashshashin, were a militant Islamic sect founded in the ninth century when Yemeni Shiite Hasan-I Sabbah led them in their mission to overthrow the Suni Muslims by killing off their leaders. The name Hashshashin, meaning 'hashish-eaters', was given to them by their enemies. The word 'assassin' was first recorded in English in 1603 and is now used to describe a hired killer, usually with a political target.

As a boy, Lance had dreamt of becoming a spy or a highly trained assassin. He still couldn't work out how he'd ended up in telesales.

Au fait

informed (French)

In French, this expression can mean 'by the way', but if it is embedded within the line '*être au fait de*' it means 'to be informed about', or 'up to a respectable level in'. There are, of course, many synonymous phrases in English, such as 'conversant in', 'up-to-date with' and 'abreast of', but somehow announcing that you're 'au fait' with all the latest developments sounds infinitely more impressive.

Deborah would have liked a promotion but there seemed to be only one route to the top, and she'd never been au fait with golfing terminology.

Auto-da-fé

act of faith (Portuguese)

The phrase comes from the Spanish Inquisition and describes a public ceremony, which included a procession, mass and a sermon, before the sentences of condemned heretics were read out by the Grand Inquisitor. In English the term is used primarily in art to describe an image of a heretic being burned at the stake, although in fact the executions didn't take place until the following day. It can also mean suicide by fire.

'Lot three is an oil painting depicting an auto-da-fé in Plaza Mayor in Madrid, circa 1683.'

Avalanche

snow slide (Romansch)

Romansch, closely related to French, is the least commonly spoken of Switzerland's four native languages and is thought to have come from the vulgar Latin spoken by the Roman settlers in that area. In the high Swiss Alps sudden movements of ice and snow are common, and sixteenth-century English-speaking visitors to the region brought the Romansch word for them home. We now use the word figuratively for any overwhelming deluge.

'I'd love to join you for lunch, sweetie, you know I would, but I'm trapped under an avalanche of fan mail – it seems my jam-tart juggling act went down rather well.'

Baksheesh

gift (Persian)

The most direct English equivalent is 'tip', but 'baksheesh' has a much more intricate meaning depending on the context in which it is used. In the Middle East and South Asia, the word originally meant a charitable donation – alms paid to a beggar, or an offering to the gods. It is still used imploringly by Arab beggars: *'Baksheesh, effendi?'* In modern usage it refers more often to an extra payment to taxi drivers, hoteliers, waiters and doormen. In the West it has developed somewhat shady undertones and occupies the territory somewhere between a tip and a bribe.

'Why don't you give him a little something to oil the wheels? I've heard a bit of baksheesh goes a long way around here.'

Bandana

to tie (Hindi, via Sanskrit)

The tie-dying technique used to decorate scarves and handkerchiefs in India is called '*bandhana*'. The anglicized 'bandana' was incorporated into the English language during the days of the British Raj, when these tie-dyed scarves were worn around the necks and waists of English masters. Bandana has since come to mean any triangular scarf worn round the neck or head, tie-dyed or not, though they're now more popular with wrestlers and cowboys than the English aristocracy.

It was rodeo day and Hoyt wasn't taking any chances – he'd been up all night sewing his initials on to his lucky bandana.

Bazaar

marketplace (Persian)

The first bazaars were established in the Middle East in around the fourth century and the word is thought to come from '*baha-char*', which means the place of prices in the Middle Persian writing system Pahlavi. Crusaders from Italy got their first introduction to the Middle East in the tenth century and borrowed the word as '*bazzara*', and it is probably through this European route that it came to be used in English.

'Oh, Marni, I just love your gem-encrusted sandals! I must have a pair – please don't tell me you found them in some untrace-able bazaar in the depths of Morocco.'

Berserk
bear shirt (Old Norse)

He'll just have to wait like everyone else.

In the ninth century the Vikings used the word to describe their ferocious warriors, who wore bearskins instead of armour. 'Berserkers' worked themselves into a frenzy before battle – some historians have suggested that they ate hallucinogenic mushrooms to heighten their rage – thus taking on the bear's bloodthirsty fury. It wasn't until a thousand years after the Viking invasions that the word appeared in English; Sir Walter Scott was one of the first to put it in print in his 1822 novel *The Pirate*. We still use it to mean dangerously violent, but it can also indicate a much milder angry outburst, or any kind of wild, unrestrained behaviour.

'Don't let your father catch you going out like that – he'll go berserk if he sees the length of your skirt.'

Bête noire

black beast (French)

Think of the person or thing that you most loathe and detest: he, she or it is your very own 'bête noire'. The term was originally reserved for mortal enemies or the stuff of your most terrifying nightmares – the sorts of things you might find in Room 101 in George Orwell's *1984*. But in recent times it has been diluted to mean any person or thing that you find personally troublesome or irritating, like a more universally applicable version of 'pet hate'. It's also a common way of referring to a sports team's biggest rival.

For two and a half hours Melissa kept her eyes firmly glued to her magazine, she liked to relax while she had her highlights done – chatty hairdressers were her bête noire.

Bijou

jewel (French)

The French term comes from the Breton word '*bizou*', which means 'ring for the finger'. By the mid sixteenth century, the French had replaced the 'z' with a 'j' and adopted it for any small gem or jewel, and by the late seventeenth century it had hopped across the Channel. In English its meaning has expanded still further to cover any exquisite and stylish little thing; today we use it to describe everything from jewels and restaurants to boutiques, hotels and even cars.

'Now, this flat is simply fantastic; less discerning buyers might say it's on the pokey side but personally I think it's wonderfully bijou.'

Bimbo

baby boy (Italian, from '*bambino*')

A bimbo is a clueless young woman who has plenty of sex appeal but not much in the brains department. Interestingly, the word is actually a contraction of the Italian for baby boy, '*bambino*', rather than the feminine version, '*bambina*'; early English usage was reserved for brainless men, but it quickly became more common as a description of a vacuous but pretty female. In the US and Britain the term can also infer a rampant sexual appetite. A jealous wife might use it to refer to a woman who she thinks is trying to seduce her husband.

'I'm sorry, Simon, we'll have to leave. I can't sit here with that bimbo batting her eyelashes at you.'

❦

Blasé

indifferent (French)

31

This word invokes a world-weary disinterest or nonchalance that comes about through over-exposure or over-indulgence. '*Blaser*' means to satiate, and may have come to French via the Middle Dutch word '*blasen*' – to blow up or swell. So someone who is blasé about something has had such a fill of it that they feel bloated and lose interest in it completely.

> *By the time she reached the eighth gallery Matilda was feeling blasé about the Old Masters and was much more interested in finding the coffee shop.*

Blitz

lightning war (German, from '*Blitzkrieg*')

A '*Blitzkrieg*' is a lightning-fast attack (from '*Blitz*' lightning, and '*Krieg*' war), the tactical opposite to '*Stellungskrieg*' ('*Stellung*' meaning position), which is warfare from prepared positions, such as trenches or fortifications. In a 1938 German military journal it is defined as a 'strategic attack' employing tanks, aircraft and airborne troops, but official use of the term by the German forces during the war was rare. The sustained aerial bombardment of Britain by the Nazis from September 1940 to May 1941 became known as the Blitz. Modern usage is less specific and can refer to anything done with vigour and speed.

> '*For the perfect winter soup just chop the leftovers from your Christmas dinner, blitz them together with some stock in the food processor, and there you have it!*'

Bon mot

right word (French)

In English, a 'bon mot' is a quip or witty remark. The phrase crossed over from France in around 1730 and became a fashionable way to describe the clever and amusing asides that entertained eighteenth-century high society. Oscar Wilde was later famous for peppering his plays with them. Sadly, many genuinely funny bons mots have been turned into clichés through over-use. The worst examples of these tend to be alcohol-related and can be found adorning the walls and menus of chain wine bars.

'If you spent as much time studying as you dedicate to delivering bons mots to your classmates, Stevens, you might one day be able to graduate.'

Bona fide

in good faith (Latin)

The original definition still stands in legal terminology, where an agreement or contract signed in good faith is said to be 'bona fide', but in everyday use the phrase has become interchangeable with the word 'genuine' and is usually used to describe a person or thing whose authenticity can be trusted. The plural also refers to the documentation that proves legitimacy, so an employer might ask to see an applicant's bona fides before offering them a job.

'Ladies and gentlemen, boys and girls, prepare to be amazed – may I proudly present Bernice, our bona fide bearded lady.'

Bonhomie

simple good-heartedness (French)

'Bonhomie' is the quality of good-natured friendliness – the term might be applied to someone who enjoys amiable conversation and has an affable disposition. The phrase first appeared in English literature in the mid 1800s and is still used in reference to warm, outgoing people, often men. Its absence in a person is also often noted as a subtle way of conveying when someone is somewhat cold and unfriendly.

Ted and Mary were dreading their dinner with the Joneses; Mr Jones wasn't exactly known for his bonhomie and Mrs Jones usually loitered in the kitchen quietly quaffing the cooking wine.

Bordello

brothel (Italian)

Though English speakers have borrowed this word from Italy, its true origins are Germanic – '*borde*' meant hut, which became the Old French word '*bordel*'. In modern use 'bordello' is an alternative word for brothel. The word is thought to date back to the late sixteenth century. Despite its link to the oldest profession, it wasn't used in the modern sense until around 1850. In recent years its meaning has mellowed still further and it is now sometimes used to describe a type of opulent interior design, there are even a few Italian restaurants called 'Il Bordello'.

'I thought we'd go for a bordello feel in this room, Deirdre; lots of velvet drapes and candelabra.'

Bourgeois

middle or merchant class (French)

This word comes from the old French '*burgeis*', which meant a townsperson. It has evolved as a label for the powerful strata of society whose status comes from self-made wealth rather than aristocratic lineage. Originally there was nothing negative about the label: even Karl Marx, who criticized the bourgeoisie for hypocrisy in *The Communist Manifesto*, used the term descriptively rather than pejoratively. Since then, though, it has taken on negative connotations and in English we tend to use it to mean boringly middle-of-the-road, materialistic or uncultured.

> *'We'll have to turn the invitation down, Nova, I wouldn't sit through another of those bourgeois dinner parties if my Anarchist Club membership depended on it.'*

Brio

vigour, vivacity (Italian/Spanish)

This is an Italian and Spanish word with Celtic origins; '*brigos*', from which it is derived, meant power, strength or force. It is thought to have entered the English language around the eighteenth century though the Italian musical instruction *con brio*, which means perform 'with vigour'. We now use it to describe the kind of verve and liveliness that we imagine we would feel at a Spanish fiesta after a jug or two of sangria.

'Did I tell you that Madeleine has started ballet lessons? Oh yes, she's only three but her performance of the "Teddy Bears' Picnic" was full of brio.'

Bungalow

a small house or cottage with a single storey (Hindi)

The Indian words *'bangala'* (Hindi), *'bungalow'* (Bengali), *'bangalo'* (Gujarati) all mean a thatched or tiled one-storey house surrounded by a wide veranda, sometimes with an additional attic storey. The English suburban fondness for such houses, especially near the coast, changed our landscape in the twentieth century. However, the 1968 Beatles song, 'The Continuing Story of Bungalow Bill' was inspired by the real thing when John Lennon mocked a rich American at the Maharishi's meditation camp who proudly shot a tiger. (In fairness, the young man's action may have been necessary and he never hunted again.)

With the lift broken and a ten-storey climb ahead, Arthur and Enid first conceived their dream – a bungalow by the sea.

Camaraderie

comradeship (French)

This word conveys a spirit of fellowship and trust between friends or colleagues. It has been used in English since the 1800s when it described the strong bonds that developed between those who suffered alongside each other in wartime. We still use the word to describe the good relationship fostered in the military between troops, and within any team or group of like-minded people united by a common cause.

Ever since the photocopying incident at the office Christmas party, the accounts team had been bound by a real sense of camaraderie.

Carpe diem

seize the day (Latin)

The Roman poet Horace coined this phrase in his poem 'Tu ne quaesieris' from Book 1 of *The Odes*, published in 23 BC. The poem was directed at a woman worrying about her future; its final line reads: '*Carpe diem, quam minimum credula postero*', which translates as, 'Seize the day, trusting tomorrow as little as possible.' The popularity of the phrase was renewed by the 1989 film *Dead Poets Society*, in which a teacher, played by Robin Williams, uses it to encourage his pupils to make their lives extraordinary. (See also '*Ars longa, vita brevis*'.)

At the aeroplane's hatch Brian was frozen with fear, what if the parachute failed, what if he landed in the middle of the ocean? 'Carpe diem,' he managed to whisper, and then he jumped.

Carte blanche

white or blank card (French)

This is a military term meaning surrender dating from the early 1700s, when a blank piece of paper was given to the victorious army on which they could write their terms. A carte blanche gave complete power to whomever it was given, and we still make use of this sense of the phrase today. If someone is given carte blanche, it means they have a free hand to do whatever they choose.

Sarah stared at the orange wallpaper in horror – she knew she should never have given Francisco carte blanche with the choice of decor.

Cause célèbre

famous case (French)

This phrase comes from the *Nouvelles causes célèbres*, a collection of famous French court verdicts published in 1763. The term became common in English after the false conviction of Alfred Dreyfuss, a Jewish officer of the French Army, for espionage in 1894. Still applied to court cases that incite public protest, the phrase can also be used to refer to any publicly controversial issue. Confusingly, many modern causes célèbres have supporters who are themselves famous, which has led the term to be mistakenly used for causes with celebrity backing.

> *From his cell Ernie Roberts thought he could hear the clamouring of an angry mob. For a heady moment he let himself believe it was for him, but he knew deep down that a pensions fraud case would never become a cause célèbre.*

Caveat emptor

let the buyer beware (Latin)

This phrase has stayed in the English language as a legal term; in property law it is used as a warning to potential buyers that the responsibility for checking the condition of a building lies with them. It has become an important phrase in the wider consumer market too, particularly in the purchase of second-hand goods. The word 'caveat' is also often used alone (without italics) as a noun to describe a warning, condition or restriction.

Having got her special-offer impulse purchase home, and finding that not only did it not fit, but that beige and shocking pink stripes weren't really 'her', Susan was unable to prevent the phrase 'caveat emptor' *from entering her mind.*

Cenotaph

empty tomb (French)

This word entered the French language from the Latin '*cenotaphium*', which in turn took it from the Greek words '*kenos*', meaning empty, and '*taphos*', meaning tomb. A cenotaph is a monument to the dead whose bodies are either lost or buried elsewhere. The large numbers of unmarked graves, and enormous numbers of soldiers and sailors with no known grave, after the First World War led to the construction of cenotaphs across the world to honour the dead. The Tombs of the Unknown Soldiers in the US and France, and Britain's national war memorial, which is simply called the Cenotaph, are the best-known examples.

Crowds gather at the Cenotaph on Remembrance Sunday to remember the British fallen heroes of both World Wars and other conflicts of the twentieth and twenty-first centuries.

C'est la vie

that's life (French)

This phrase originated in France, where it was said with a sigh after something difficult or disappointing had happened to mean 'that's just the way life goes'. It is still used in France in this context, though these days it is considered old-fashioned. In English the phrase has stuck, but it does have to compete with such modern variations as 'that's the way the cookie crumbles' and the somewhat more prosaic 'shit happens'.

'Come on, Tony, you've got to put that French girl out of your mind and move on.'
'I know, Dave, but everywhere I turn there's something French that reminds me of her.'
'C'est la vie, I'm afraid.'

Chagrin

distress (French)

The origins of this word, which is used to convey a sense of aggravation, sheepishness or displeasure, are widely disputed. Some etymologists believe that it comes from a rough leather of the same name (English 'shagreen'), while others say it comes from a French translation of the German word for hangover – *Katzenjammer*. Most likely, though, it comes from a Germanic word *grami*, meaning sorrow or trouble, as the earliest English usage was for anxiety and sadness. Nowadays the word is used in English to signify slight disappointment, tinged with irritation.

Malcolm had planned to pass the shop-bought salmon terrine off as his own creation, but much to his chagrin Stephanie sauntered into the kitchen just as he was taking it out of the packet.

Cherchez la femme
look for the woman (French)

This phrase was taken from the 1854 book *Les Mohicans de Paris* by French author Alexandre Dumas *père* (not to be confused with his son, also named Alexandre Dumas). He was best known for his historical adventure fiction and this phrase conveys the view that a woman was almost always behind the misadventures of men. It retains this meaning in modern use, though sometimes with sardonic overtones, and it can also be used more generally to encourage someone to look for the underlying cause of a problem.

Charles let out a gasp as he opened his credit card bill. 'Cherchez la femme,' he muttered under his breath as he dialled the number of his accountant.

Chic
elegant (French)

In English, chic is synonymous with 'fashionable' and 'stylish'. It is thought to originate from a German word *Schick*, which means fitness and elegance, though the French monopoly on all things related to fashion ensured that English speakers took the fran-cophone version. It is used today to denote an outfit, object or place that exudes sophistication and style.

'I felt very out of place in my socks and comfortable sandals, I can tell you; we just weren't expecting it to be so chic.'

Chop chop

hurry (Chinese, from '*k'wâi-k'wâi*')

The phrase originated in the South China Sea, as a Pidgin English version of the Chinese term '*k'wâi-k'wâi*'. The adoption of the 'chop-chop' pronunciation was in harmony with the long-standing use of 'chop' and 'chop-up' by British seamen, with the meaning 'quick' or 'hurried'. The seafaring usage of 'chop up' referred specifically to a sudden change in the wind and the waves (hence 'choppy'). The British say 'chop-chop' when they want someone, usually a child but originally a foreign servant, to hurry up. They may also clap their hands to underscore the urgency.

Miss Brindle flared her nostrils. 'Chop-chop, girls!' she said briskly as her charges reluctantly tidied the nursery.

Chop suey

bits and pieces (Chinese, from '*tsap sui*')

Chop suey is widely believed to have been invented in America by Chinese immigrants, but seems to originate in Taishan, a district of Guangdong Province. A popular story has the dish invented during Premier Li Hongzhang's visit to the USA in 1896. His chef tried to create a dish suitable for both Chinese and American palates. When asked what food the Premier was eating, the cook found it difficult to explain and replied 'mixed pieces'.

Unfamiliar with Chinese food, Jeff said, 'I'll have whatever, bits and pieces.'
'Chop suey, excellent choice!' his host replied.

Chutney

to taste (Hindi)

The name for this sweet and spicy condiment comes from the East Indian word '*chatni*'. Traditionally reserved for special occasions because they required an intensive preparation process, chutneys began to be imported by Western countries in the late 1600s and by the nineteenth century more subtly spiced versions were being produced especially for export. We now use the word for a huge variety of preserved condiments and pickles.

The most popular stall at the town fair was always Mrs Hubbard's: people flocked from far and wide for a taste of her green tomato chutney.

———◦◉◦———

Chutzpah

audacity (Yiddish)

This comes from the Hebrew word '*hutspah*' (which is how 'chutz-pah' is pronounced), meaning insolence. It originally referred to someone who had brazenly broken the rules of respectable behaviour and was only used in a disapproving sense. In Yiddish and subsequently English, however, it can convey a quality worthy of a sort of reluctant admiration – a daring effrontery that we might describe as 'gutsy'. It might also be used today to describe the performance of a precocious musician or dancer who has delivered a challenging interpretation of a particularly difficult piece.

The President smiled as the pro-vegan protester was escorted away. Leading a live cow into Congress was a crazy idea but he couldn't help but admire the man's chutzpah.

———◦◉◦———

Cogito, ergo sum

I think, therefore I am (Latin)

This famous philosophical quotation is from René Descartes's 1673 *Discourse on Method*, in which he asserted the fact that the power of thought was proof of the existence of the self. He originally wrote it in French rather than Latin ('*Je pense, donc je suis*') so that it was accessible to a broader range of readers, but he switched to Latin in his later work *Principles of Philosophy*. Modern philosophers refer to the phrase as 'the cogito'.

'I thought I deserved a far better grade than a D for that, sir.'
'Well, that's something, Toby. Cogito, ergo sum – *take comfort from that.'*

※◦⊙◦※

Cognoscenti

those who know (Italian)

This word arrived in Italian from the Latin '*conoscere*', which means to know. The spelling we have taken on is now in fact obsolete in Italy, where '*conoscenti*' has taken its place. In English the word is usually used to describe people who are experts in the fields of art, literature or fashion, indicating a certain refinement in taste and judgement. It is also used more colloquially to describe those who are 'in the know' on any subject; a member of the cocktail cognoscenti could guide one to the perfect Manhattan, while the techno cognoscenti would lead you to the best rave.

You couldn't find leopard-print leggings that year for love nor money, for the fashion cognoscenti had bought up every last pair.

※◦⊙◦※

Compos mentis

a composed mind (Latin)

This Latin phrase has survived through both medical and legal use; in neurological terms it means sane or mentally healthy and in law it indicates that someone is of sound enough mind to stand trial. The term's opposite – non compos mentis, meaning not of sound mind, is just as frequently used in modern English to argue that a person should not be held legally responsible for their actions. This has extended in everyday use to mean anyone who through tiredness or heavy drinking isn't quite 'with it'.

'You'd better get Gavin a cab home, Lou, I don't think he's fully compos mentis.'

Confetti

sweets (Italian)

The term is the plural of '*confetto*' meaning 'candy', but the term is exclusively used in Italy for sugared almonds, which are eaten at weddings, baptisms and first communions. The British and American tradition of throwing confetti at weddings is related to the very old tradition of throwing rice, dates or nuts that may reach back beyond Ancient Rome or Egypt. It brings good luck and represents fertility and abundance. In Italy, the earliest form of confetti may have consisted of sugar-coated nuts and similar confections. In modern day, eco-sensitive times, flower petals are often preferred by licensed wedding venues but the sentiment and significance remain unchanged.

It wasn't nerves or emotions that made Stanley feel choked-up; he'd just inhaled three mouthfuls of confetti.

Connoisseur

expert (French)

Most members of the cognoscenti (see above) could be referred to as connoisseurs. The word comes from '*connaître*', which means 'to be acquainted with', and is used to describe a person who has a specialized knowledge of a subject or thing. True connoisseurs are found mainly in the art world – collectors, curators or art critics. In the eighteenth century the word was used to describe any person of taste and nowadays it also applies to knowledgeable devotees of everything from real ale to contemporary Dutch sculpture.

The waiter left Mr McNair to pore over the menu of single malts at his leisure – the gentleman's florid complexion marked him out as something of a whisky connoisseur.

Contretemps

against the time (French)

In the seventeenth century a contretemps was a mistimed or inopportune thrust in a fencing bout. This meaning extended in English use by around 1770 to cover any jarring mishap that was out of pace with social mores. We still use the term to describe an unexpected interruption in normal proceedings, but since the mid twentieth century it has been used more widely to mean an embarrassing set-to, or minor skirmish.

Hugh felt edgy as he arrived at the restaurant. The parking ticket was stuffed uncomfortably into his back pocket and he couldn't get his contretemps with the traffic warden out of his head.

Cordon bleu

blue ribbon (French)

The Blue Ribbon was awarded by the sixteenth-century Bourbon kings to knights of the highest order. The term was incorporated into English in the 1720s for noblemen and the phrase has since become an accolade for top-quality cooking. An 1827 cookbook called *Le Cordon bleu ou Nouvelle cuisinière bourgeoise* was the first to use the phrase in this context and when a branch of Le Cordon Bleu school was founded in London in 1933, the phrase became part of the English culinary dictionary, and synonymous with high-class cuisine.

Peter stood back and admired his creation. It wasn't exactly cordon bleu but it didn't look too bad now he'd sliced off the burnt bits.

Coup de grâce

blow of mercy (French)

This is a final death blow that ends the suffering of someone who is wounded. On the battlefield it referred specifically to a bullet shot to the heart or head. These days we also use it to describe the final stroke of misfortune that results in the demise of a business or relationship, but in our attempt at an authentic French accent we often mispronounce it. By leaving out the final 's' sound, it sounds like we're saying '*cou de gras*' or 'neck of fat', which doesn't have quite the same pathos.

The relationship had been on the rocks for a while but Leo's decision to watch the football on Valentine's Day was the coup de grâce.

Crime passionnel

crime of passion (French)

Until the 1970s French juries were allowed to take into account the circumstances surrounding a murder. If someone had killed for love or out of jealousy, rather than as part of a premeditated plan, jurors often found reason to acquit them. A case like this was known as a *crime passionnel* and the term became common in English in 1955 during the trial of Ruth Ellis, who in a jealous rage shot her unfaithful lover five times outside a London pub. She became the last woman in Britain to receive the death penalty.

Sharon wondered if she could get away with claiming it was a crime passionnel, *but the chances of anyone believing she was in love with her neighbour's dog seemed slim.*

Curriculum vitae

course of life (Latin)

This is a summary of everything we have achieved educationally and professionally in our lives up to the present day. Most of us have written one at some point and many of us may have read through a selection of other people's when looking for a new employee. Though the full translation sounds rather poetic, most curricula vitae, CVs, or résumés in the US, reduce the course of life to its barest shell, leaving room only for word processing qualifications and spurious 'hobbies' such as relaxing and socializing with friends.

> *Caitlyn seems a lively girl but I don't think we can possibly employ her. When I asked for her curriculum vitae she said, 'Five foot four, 34D.'*

Cushy

easy/pleasant (Urdu, from '*khushi*')

The Urdu word '*khushi*' meaning happy, easy or soft, was adopted as 'cushy' by members of the British Army serving in India in the late nineteenth century. It was considered slang then, as it is today, and used to describe a situation that is not only highly agreeable, but also considered lucky; the sort of position that we might describe as 'nice work if you can get it'. In the US the term is also employed to describe a comfortably shaped person.

> *'And you get paid just to look after someone else's house while they're on holiday? That's a bit cushy, isn't it?'*

-⊶⊙⊙⊶-

De rigueur

necessary (French)

Like so many English phrases that relate to etiquette and fashion, we borrowed this term from the French. If something is de rigueur it is necessary according to the strict codes of protocol, despite not being enshrined by an official rule or law. The term was especially useful in the rigidly rule-bound Victorian era, but since then it has also come to mean anything that is in line with the latest trends.

Charlotte spent the last few moments before her guests arrived decanting her supermarket-brand coffee into an unmarked tin; along with organic vegetables, fair trade coffee had become de rigueur at dinner parties these days.

-⊶⊙⊙⊶-

De trop

in excess (French)

This phrase means 'too much' and can be used in two ways. Its original meaning in English was simply too many, or a superfluous amount, and it is still used in this way to point out – in a delicate, French way, of course – that something is over the top or beyond the bounds of good taste. It is also used when a person's presence isn't welcome, like when your boyfriend's best mate tags along on every date.

'I thought wearing a cloak and sword with his dinner jacket was rather de trop.'

Debacle

collapse (French)

This word comes from '*débâcler*', which means to unbar or break loose, but in both French and English, its true definition is a catastrophic failure or collapse. It originally referred to the caving-in of a physical structure, like a roof, or to flooding caused by the break-up of ice in a river, and also to a terrible defeat in battle. Over time it has become a useful way of describing less dramatic defeats as terrible muddles and failure, such as sports matches where one team received a drubbing, or for sometimes ludicrous political or organizational failures.

Kelvin once had his hopes pinned on the top job, but his career had never quite recovered from the 'pay rise for politicians' debacle.

Decree nisi

unless (Latin)

This phrase means simply not final or absolute, but it has retained its place in English as a legal term. A decree nisi is a ruling by the court that won't come into effect until a certain condition has been met – usually that there are no further presentations of relevant material to the court. We use the term to refer to a conditional divorce that will become absolute after the passing of a set amount of time, unless there is just cause to modify it.

Nicole gave a little skip of joy as she left the solicitor's office. The judge had issued a decree nisi and in six weeks and a day she would be free.

---◦◦◦---

Déjà vu

already seen (French)

This term is used to describe the feeling of having already been through an experience you are actually having for the first time. Its earliest use was in a French translation of Sigmund Freud's *Psychopathology of Everyday Life*, published in 1901, in which he suggested that the feeling corresponded to the memory of a subconscious daydream. We still use it to describe this as yet unexplained phenomenon, but a sense of déjà vu is also now used when an event feels similar to something that has happened in the past.

Homeowners watched interest rates rise with an unnerving sense of déjà vu.

---◦◦◦---

Delicatessen

fine foods or delicacies (German)

This word has its origins in the Latin word '*delicatus*', which means 'pleasure-giving', but arrived in English via the German '*Delikatessen*', which described ready-to-eat foods such as cold meats, cheeses and salads. In English the term is almost exclusively used to describe not the foodstuffs themselves but the shops that sell them. Colloquially known as 'delis', these are often Italian, rather than German, and are characterized by the smell of freshly roasted coffee and vats of garlic-infused olives.

There was only one person to blame for the failure of Jenna's diet – the proprietor of her local delicatessen, who, she felt sure, laced his chocolate brownies with some sort of highly addictive chemical.

———◦☙◦———

Demi-monde

half-world (French)

An 1855 play called *Le Demi-Monde* by Alexandre Dumas *fils* gave the French this word for mistresses. It describes a half-world on the fringes of eighteenth-century society inhabited by courtesans. Mistresses were an accepted part of upper-class life in both France and Britain and the term soon migrated across the Channel, though its use in this context faded in the twentieth century as the women's rights movement grew. It was subsequently used to describe a world of penniless bohemian artists and those on the edges of respectable society.

> *'That's it, I'm going back to the day job. Ventriloquism is all I've ever wanted to do but I can't live in this demi-monde a moment longer.'*

———◦☙◦———

Denouement

an untying (French)

Have you got to the bit where the policeman confesses?

After the climax of a story, there are usually a few loose ends to tie up, this is the denouement. Confusingly perhaps, since the French word means untying, but whichever tying metaphor you feel most comfortable with, the final outcome is the same – a neatening up of a plot's complexities. As with so many theatrical methods, Shakespeare is the master of the denouement and most of his dramas conclude with false identities being uncovered, justice being done and everyone getting married.

'I just can't follow these murder mysteries; I usually just nap through until the denouement.'

Derrière

behind (French)

The bottom is one of the few parts of the body for which we have a plethora of words. Many of these arrived in the English language in the seventeenth and eighteenth centuries, either as slang or as euphemisms, and 'behind' was among them. Exactly how or why this was translated to 'derrière' is unclear. It could have been because few people, especially servants and children, spoke French. Or perhaps it was felt that the Frenchness took the edge off its vulgarity and lent the term a certain Continental dignity that 'arse', 'bum' and 'backside' lack.

'I don't know what I'm going to do with that budgie, I bent down to pick up some seeds that had dropped from its cage and it leant through the bars and pecked me on the derrière.'

Déshabillé (also dishabille)

undressed (French)

Dating back to the seventeenth century in English usage, this word is used to convey the state of being either very casually dressed or only partially clothed. In settings where propriety required a certain dress-code, it would have referred to an inappropriately informal and careless way of dressing, which gave rise to the additional meaning of disordered thinking. These days it is still used to mean undressed, and can also mean a garment that you wear when mostly undressed, like a nightdress or underwear.

Things had been strained in the Mortimer household since Mr Mortimer had been caught in a state of déshabillé in the church hall with two members of the WI.

Deus ex machina

god from the machinery (Latin)

This describes a plot device used in Greek tragedy in which seemingly impossible situations were resolved by actors playing gods being lowered onto the stage by a crane and whisking everyone off to a happy ending. The phrase was first used by Horace in his *Ars Poetica*, in which he warned his fellow Roman poets against resorting to such unimaginative methods in their craft. Over time its meaning evolved to encompass any sudden and unrealistically simple external solution to a complex problem in a narrative, and critics still use the phrase in this way today.

> *'A sentimental novel with a* deus ex machina *so clunky that you could almost hear the ropes creaking.'*

Diaspora

scattering (Greek)

This comes from the Greek word '*diaspeirein*', which means to spread about in the sense of sowing or scattering, but in references as far back as the Old Testament, it is used specifically to describe the body of Jews living outside of Israel after their exile to Babylonia in the sixth century BC. Jewish communites around the world are still referred to in this way, though the word is also now applied to any dispersion of people or entities that originate in one fixed place.

Union Jacks and cafes serving egg and chips are the usual calling cards of the British diaspora in the Mediterranean.

Diktat

something dictated (German)

A punitive decree issued to a defeated nation is called a 'diktat', since its terms are dictated by the victor. The 1919 Treaty of Versailles was called 'The Diktat' by the Germans because they had no option but to accept its damaging and humiliating terms. Its use became widespread in English from that point onward and we now use it as a label for any harsh order or compulsory instruction issued by an individual or organization in authority.

A collective sigh of resignation echoed through the staffroom as the Headmaster delivered his latest diktat.

Dilettante

one who delights (Italian, from '*dilettare*')

This is an example of a word that starts out with a friendly, positive meaning but after three centuries of use has ended up with a negative one. In the early 1700s it meant someone who took delight in fine art, without becoming an expert in it – an enthusiastic dabbler, as we might say now. No harm in that, you might think, but the word began to turn; the lack of expertise it implied became a suggestion of unprofessionalism and superficiality and by the twentieth century it defined someone lacking in skill and commitment and possibly even a bit useless.

> *At first he'd seemed like the perfect man for the job, but he was exposed as a dilettante when a dog-eared copy of* The Bluffer's Guide to Antiques *fell out of his briefcase.*

Diva

goddess (Italian)

The term now applies to any well-known female performer or prima donna, and, more generally, to an acclaimed female in any sphere of endeavour. Pejoratively the word also means a person who considers herself (or by extension himself) more important than others and becomes angry or petulant when their standards or demands are not met. The literal meaning of the term is 'goddess', the feminine of the Latin word *divus*, 'god'. Diva even features as a girl's name (divine one or goddess), which might be hard for a girl to live up to.

> *Margery considered herself a diva, so when her lotus-blossom throat linctus wasn't in the dressing room you could hear her complaining right across the village hall.*

※

Dolce vita
sweet life (Italian)

A life of luxury and self-indulgence has been described in English as '*la dolce vita*' since the 1960 release of a film of that name by Federico Fellini. The film documented the opulence and material-ism of modern Rome at the start of Europe's most liberal decade and painted the city as a hub of romantic decadence. Originally the phrase was employed ironically to describe a morally flawed way of life, but in recent years its meaning has softened into something more literal and 'ah, *la dolce vita*' can now be heard in place of the English phrase 'this is the life'.

> *Mick and Lorraine arrived at the airport with three hours to spare. They wanted their two weeks living* la dolce vita *to start as soon as they'd got through check-in and they needed plenty of time to drink duty-free champagne.*

※

Doolally
camp fever (Urdu, from '*Deolali*')

In 1861 the British army established a military base at Deolali, about a hundred miles north of Mumbai, that was used as a transit camp for soldiers who'd completed their tour of duty and were waiting for a boat back home or were on their way up-country. The wait often lasted for months and in the boredom and heat many men began to behave oddly. Troops would say, 'He's got the Doolally tap,' of anyone who seemed a bit mad; tap translates as fever. We now use the phrase 'gone doolally' to describe someone who is behaving strangely.

> *'Sorry I'm late, Margaret! I've gone completely doolally; I thought I'd lost my car keys and finally found them in the fruit bowl when I went to pick up an apple!'*

Doppelgänger

double goer (German)

In psychiatry, a 'doppelgänger' is a delusion of a human double, but the word long pre-dates modern psychiatric analysis. It referred originally to a ghostly phantom double, the sight of which was considered a bad omen. Romantic poet Percy Bysshe Shelley saw his in Italy in 1822, pointing solemnly out to sea. Soon afterwards Shelley drowned in a sailing accident. Now the word is used for someone who looks strangely similar to yourself or another person, or for your avatar in alternative-reality online games, where you can create your very own virtual doppelgänger.

'Are you sure we haven't met before? If not I think I'm acquainted with your doppelgänger, she was on the same cruise as us last year in the Canary Islands.'

Double entendre

double understanding (French)

This expression is now obsolete in France, where '*double sens*' or '*double entente*' are used in its place, but in English it retains its original definition as a phrase that has an innocent first meaning and a saucy or ironic secondary meaning. Such phrases have been a pillar of English wordplay since Shakespeare's time, when ribald humour was the order of the day, and are still widely used in comedy today.

'I made the most embarrassing double entendre in the super-market yesterday; the cashier handed me a carrier bag and I asked him if he had a big one!'

Doyen/ne

senior member of a group (French)

This word came to French from the Latin '*decanus*', which means commander of ten men and from which we also get the word 'clean'. Though this usage has long been obsolete, the modern meaning of the most senior or eldest male member of a group is probably derived from this ancient definition. Nowadays we are more meritocratic in our use of the word, the feminine version doyenne is just as frequently used and both words describe the most successful, most admired or most influential figures in their field.

Ladies and gentlemen, would you please welcome to the stage our star speaker, Mr Colin Muggeridge, the doyen of double-glazing.'

Du jour

of the day (French)

This is used in English in two ways – in the context of a dish on a menu to mean something freshly prepared and available on that day only, such as a soup *du jour*, or in more recent use, to signify something that is 'very now' or of the moment, with the implication that its popularity will be short-lived. An extended version of the phrase – *femme du jour* – might also be used to describe the latest girlfriend of a man with a commitment problem.

Monique had slept through her alarm on the morning of the Paris Fashion Show, but she thanked her lucky stars as she caught sight of the catwalk. Un-brushed bed hair was apparently the look *du jour.*

Dungarees

thick cotton cloth/overalls (Hindi)

During the days of British colonial rule in India, sails and tents were made from a thick, hard-wearing cotton cloth called '*dungri*'. It was shipped from India to England in great quantities during the eighteenth century when it picked up an additional syllable and turned into 'dungaree'. The durability of the fabric made it ideal for work overalls and the trousers with a bib and shoulder straps that we know as dungarees were born.

'I'm sorry, sweetie, but dungarees are not a good look for you; you need a bit of a ska band look to pull them off these days, and your style is more Bananarama.'

Eau de toilette

toilet water (French)

Not that kind of toilet . . . in the seventeenth century a *toilette* was a cloth cover for a ladies' dressing table, having originally meant a cloth cover as wrapper for clothes. By extension '*toilette*' came to mean the process of dressing, and later of washing, thus eau de toilette is a scent. It differs from perfume only in that the percentage of aromatic compounds used to make it is slightly lower, making it lighter and less expensive. We use the French term not only because it sounds less unsanitary but because during the seventeenth and eighteenth centuries, when infrequent bathing made perfumes most popular, France was the centre of a prospering perfume and cosmetic trade.

With the boiler still broken Elspeth hadn't bathed in over a week, but it was amazing what a damp cloth and a spritz of eau de toilette could do to give the impression of cleanliness.

Éclat

splinter, brilliance, burst (French)

The original meaning of this word in English was notoriety or scandal. It comes from the Old French word '*esclater*' – to burst out, like a skeleton from a closet, perhaps. Now though it is firmly lodged in our vocabulary as a description of a scintillating performance worthy of great acclaim. Women may also recognize it from the tube of Lancôme's 'Touche Éclat' in their make-up bag, though brilliant might not be how most of us would describe even the best-concealed of under-eye shadows.

Leonard packed his karaoke machine away with pride. He could tell from the open mouths in the audience that he'd given a performance of great éclat.

Élan

leap, fervour, burst (French)

One of the French meanings of this word is synonymous with 'éclat' above – a burst or surge (of activity). In English, however, they are often used together to convey panache and flair. But next to élan, éclat can seem brash and flashy, élan is éclat's sophisticated older brother, redolent of a refined, understated elegance. It comes from the Old French '*eslan*', which means rush, and is most commonly used in English to describe a kind of ardent vigour and zeal.

The students seemed to be waving a different banner every day, but fought every battle with equal élan, they were rebels with multiple causes.

Embonpoint

in good condition, fleshy (French, from '*en bon point*')

This word sums up the way our ideals about body shape have changed over the centuries. Its literal translation means pleasingly plump, like the voluptuous women Rubens was painting in the early seventeenth century, which was around the time the word was first used. In women, this quality of desirable fleshiness is often accompanied by a heaving bosom, and the word is still used euphemistically to refer to this most peachy part of the female body.

'The two leads were so ill-matched in physical stature that at one point the tenor nearly disappeared into the soprano's generous embonpoint.'

En masse

in mass (French)

This term is so similar in French to its English translation that it seems strange that we felt the need to adopt it, but around 1800, with protest marches from the cotton spinners, the Chartists and the Anti-Corn-Law League on the horizon, the British borrowed from the French, who had already established themselves as the leading authority on civil unrest. We still use it to indicate a group moving as one, but the context is often less worthy; these days we're more likely to head en masse to the bar after work.

There were a few pink cheeks in the capital yesterday as four thousand naturists marched through the city en masse.

Enfant terrible

terrible child (French)

Though not often used literally, this term can be applied to children who humiliate their parents by making loud, embarrassingly candid declarations in public. Usually though, it is reserved for radical, unorthodox adults, mostly in the art world, whose outrageous behaviour shocks and unnerves mainstream society. The phrase was coined by Thomas Jefferson to describe the headstrong architect Pierre Charles L'Enfant, who was commissioned to build the United States Capitol in Washington DC, but was fired after eleven months for tearing down the home of the city's commissioner to build a boulevard.

Reuben had tried everything to get himself known as the new enfant terrible of the art world; he'd even pickled his own hand in formaldehyde, but so far no one seemed to have noticed.

Ennui

boredom (French)

We claimed this word from the French in the eighteenth century when cultivated society needed a term that distinguished the listless dissatisfaction felt by the elite from the bog standard boredom of the man on the street. In 1809 it became the title of a novel by pre-eminent writer Maria Edgeworth in which she critiqued the lethargy of the leisured upper classes. We still use the word to describe a profound sort of boredom today.

'I don't think I can ever turn the television on again, Lucinda; the vacuous nonsense they show these days overcomes me with ennui.'

Entre nous

between ourselves (French)

There is something about the French language that makes it seem just right for secrets, perhaps it's the relaxed Gallic attitude to illicit liaisons, or the fact that a smattering of French while revealing some hush-hush little morsel makes us come over all French resistance, whatever it is, *entre nous*, which dates back to the 1680s in its homeland, has become an almost obligatory precursor to any juicy revelation. It means that what you're about to say must stay between you and the recipient of your information.

'Marion? It's me – Barbara. Meet me in the coffee shop at three fifteen, usual table. And come alone; I've got something to tell you that's strictly entre nous.'

Erratum

mistake (Latin)

This comes from the Latin verb '*errāre*', which means to stray or err, and is used specifically in printing and, more recently, in computer programming. It refers to an error that has been formally noted by editors after the completion of the production process when the text cannot be changed. Rather than incur the expense of reprinting a whole run of books an erratum, or a list of errata can be printed on a separate page and bound into the book.

It had taken Richard Pratt sixteen years to complete his memoir of Fluffy the Peruvian guinea pig, so it was with some frustration that the final page of his manuscript contained that dreaded word 'erratum'.

Ersatz

replacement (German)

This comes from '*ersetzen*', which means to replace, and in Germany the term is straightforward; in sports an '*Ersatzspieler*' is a substitute player. But the word picked up some negativity on its route into English. During World War I, when Allied blockades prevented the delivery of goods to Germany, substitutes had to be found for the basic essentials. Coffee, for instance, was made using roasted grains rather than coffee beans. The practice resumed in World War II, when Allied prisoners of war who were given this tasteless '*Ersatzkaffee*' took the word home with them for any inferior substitution or imitation.

> *'Pass me that glass of champagne quickly, Gloria! I think that last canapé was some kind of dreadful ersatz caviar.'*

Esprit de corps

group spirit (French)

Used especially in reference to members of a military unit, this word conveys the pride and sense of unity that arises in teams of people who are working closely together. Camaraderie (see p.36) is a crucial ingredient in it, as is a shared sense of purpose and commitment to reaching a goal. Regrettably, in recent years the term has been appropriated by corporate team building gurus who try to drum up this now elusive force with orienteering exercises and games of Twister.

> *'OK, everybody, the aim is to hold the balloon under your chin and pass it on to the person next to you without it popping. This is really going to generate some* esprit de corps, *I can just feel it!'*

Et cetera

and the rest (Latin)

This is a remarkably efficient phrase that is usually shortened to 'etc.' with a point at the end. It allows the user to give the gist of their meaning without having to list every example they can think of. Usually 'etc.' is used when the list of things that is too lengthy to write in full has some pattern or order, such as a group of ingredients or items you need to remember to pack for your holiday. It is also used informally in the titles of European monarchs to denote that the number of grand titles is simply too long to list.

'There will be four days of camping so everyone needs wet weather gear: waterproofs, wellington boots etc., etc.'

Eureka

I have found it (Greek)

Archimedes's famous exclamation on discovering how to measure the volume of an irregular object has been in our vocabulary for centuries as an expression of discovery. The legendary Greek scholar reportedly realized while stepping into a bath that water displacement could be used to measure the volume of an irregular object. He was so excited by his discovery that he apparently jumped straight back out of the bath and ran naked onto the streets of Syracuse.

'Eureka! That's the turning we need ahead on the left, Jennifer. I told you I knew where we were going!'

———❦———

Ex libris

from the books of (Latin)

This term has been used since Roman times to denote the ownership of a book. It refers to the label or mark within the cover of a book that details the library or individual that it belongs to. The earliest recorded *ex libris* dates from around 1400 BC and proclaims ownership by the Egyptian Pharaoh Amenophis III. Paper labels or ink stamps are still used for this purpose today, though the phrase is mostly used by collectors and librarians.

> *'This is a lovely present, James, but are you sure you bought it? It's just that the* ex libris *says it's the property of the public library.'*

———❦———

Exposé

exposed (French)

Originally used to describe a verbal or written explanation that 'exposed' the reasons behind a decision, particularly in diplomatic circles, 'exposé' is now used for a report that unveils the truth about an individual or organization. Modern day exposés usually appear in tabloid newspapers; their subjects are celebrities, politicians or public bodies and what they expose is often a scandalous secret or discreditable fact.

Annabelle felt betrayed, heartbroken and a bit strapped for cash, so she decided to sell her story to the press; a lurid exposé would be the perfect revenge.

Factotum

do everything (Latin)

This word originally described a servant employed to do a range of different kinds of work; usually someone employed by a family to run the household. By the sixteenth century the meaning had shifted to mean someone who gets everywhere and knows everything, and it had the same negative connotations as the modern equivalent 'busybody'. Now though, some of the original sense of the word has returned and we use it to describe someone who can turn their hand to anything, a jack of all trades or general assistant.

'I like to keep my options open work wise. When I filled in that careers assessment form it came back with two options, fraudster or factotum: I kept my nose clean and chose the latter.'

Fait accompli

accomplished fact (French)

Though French in origin, this phrase was introduced to our language by an Englishman, in a travel book about Spain. Richard

Ford's *Handbook for Travellers in Spain* was published in 1845 to great literary acclaim. In it, he describes a previously settled fact as a fait accompli and the phrase took its place in the English lexicon. It is still very commonly used to describe decisions that have been made before those affected can have an input, or to situations that are irreversible.

> *If there was one role that Darius Donovan hoped he'd never play it was the back end of the cow, but by the time he arrived for casting it was already a fait accompli.*

Faux pas

wrong step (French)

It's heartening to know that cultural slip-ups occur even in sophisticated French society. Perhaps to comfort ourselves with a reminder of this fact, English speakers have adopted the French phrase for them. A 'wrong step' is the perfect way to describe such mishaps, as they usually leave us metaphorically stumbling, cheeks flushed with embarrassment and confusion, until we find our feet again. A visit abroad is the primary setting for these incidents, since social mores differ so dramatically between cultures.

'He asked me to pass the bread; I had my fork in my right hand so I used my left and the whole room went quiet – I still don't know why but somehow I'd made a terrible faux pas.'

Femme fatale

deadly woman (French)

The dangerously seductive female has been a figure in the popular imagination since the days of ancient folklore. Salome, Cleopatra and even Eve have all been retrospectively labelled as such, but this term didn't come into use in English until around 1912, when women were beginning to challenge Victorian notions of female propriety. It is now used mostly to describe sexually powerful female figures in film and literature, including spies or assassins, who use their charm and beauty to ensnare men, or more collo- quially for women who dress in an overtly seductive way.

By day Laura-Jane was a sweet, cardigan-wearing schoolteacher, but by night she was a leather-clad femme fatale.

Feng shui

wind and water (Mandarin Chinese)

'Feng shui' is the Chinese art of placing objects in patterns such as yin and yang, compass points and astrology, so that the flow of 'chi' (life force), is healthy. In the English-speaking West the term most often refers to the repositioning of furniture within a house so that the environment we live in is in line with the landscape and the movement of the earth. There are many authentic feng shui practitioners who can make these recommendations, though in recent years there has also been a proliferation of mediocre interior designers who use the word for a more generalized Chinese-style decor.

'Have you seen what Margery next door has done to her garden? It's all rock pools and bamboo shoots, very feng shui.'

Fest

festival (German)

The German word for festival, used to describe gatherings that celebrate a specific activity, has become a useful suffix in English; there are now fests of every description, from knit fests to truffle fests and chilli fests. And if a music festival gets a bit slippery underfoot, we call it a mud fest. Its use became widespread in the 1970s, possibly inspired by the growing reputation of Munich's world-famous 'Oktoberfest', a carnival of beer and bratwursts that has been running since 1810 and is attended by six million people each year.

'The frying pans are sizzling and the tasters are at the ready – it's time to declare the inaugural fish-finger fest officially open!'

Fiasco

failure or bottle (Italian)

Fiasco is in fact an Italian word used to describe a type of bottle with rope wound around the bottom, but its dual meaning of failure comes via the French phrase *'faire fiasco'*. Because it is a slang term, its origins are hazy, but one possibility stems from the phrase's earliest (and very specific) use: to describe a linguistic mistake made by Italian actors working on the French stage in the eighteenth century. The now obsolete French expression '*faire une bouteille*' which meant 'make a mistake' was probably then Italianized to '*fare fiasco*'. We still use it to mean a humiliating failure.

> *Brian checked the elastic on every team member's shorts personally. He was determined there would be no repeat of last season's wardrobe-malfunction fiasco.*

Fiesta

festival or celebration (Spanish)

I told you not to tell the chap from the tapas bar that it was a fiesta.

The Spanish know how to throw a party and, with saints' days liberally scattered throughout the Spanish calendar, there are plenty of opportunities for processions, feasts and dances. The word is used in English primarily to describe Spanish or Latin American festivals, particularly when the speaker happens to have attended one on their holidays and wants to show their friends how relaxed and Latin-spirited they are about using the local terminology.

Graham put on his papier-mâché horse's head and looked in the mirror. He felt dressed more for a freak show than a fiesta, but the parade was about to begin and Juan had insisted.

Frisson

shiver (French)

This word evolved in French from the Late Latin '*frigēre*' (to be cold), and the term applies to a sensation of fear or excitement as physically discernable as a shiver caused by a blast of cold air. Unlike a real icy shudder, though, there is always an element of pleasure in a frisson. The word arrived in English from the French in the late eighteenth century and we still use it to describe the sort of pleasing terror elicited by a good horror story, or a thrilling sexual tension.

Sally-Anne trembled as she wrote her number on the back of her shopping list. She'd felt a definite frisson with the man in the pet-food aisle and decided it was too good an opportunity to miss.

Froideur

coldness (French)

It seems somehow apt that English speakers have embraced a French word for cold superiority, given that we often view the French, or the Parisians at least, as those most likely to exhibit the trait. The word is used in both languages to describe a reserved manner or even a marked frostiness between two parties and is particularly useful in international relations, when to say outright that there is distrust or active hatred between two countries might be diplomatically uncouth.

There had been a palpable froideur *between the two women since they knocked each other unconscious while diving for the bouquet at a mutual friend's wedding.*

Frottage

rubbing (French)

The word comes from the French verb '*frotter*', to rub, and for a while it was a psychiatric name for a sexual disorder characterized by the desire to rub up against another person without their consent (now known as frotterism). It does have a more innocent meaning in the art world, where it refers to the technique for making brass rubbings, but these days it's generally reserved for the kind of consensual, through-the-clothes body-rubbing that we might otherwise be forced to call 'dry humping'.

'Sorry I was so long with the drinks; I got waylaid by a bit of dance-floor frottage.'

Furore

excitement/controversy (Italian)

In American English this word is spelt without the 'e', while the British stick to the Italian spelling, but both versions have the same meaning: a sudden excited outburst, usually by a large body of people, about something that has caused a stir. It originates from the Latin word *furor*, meaning 'a raging', but the modern usage doesn't always imply anger, just a dramatic and clamorous reaction to an event or decision.

Geraldine left the school hall feeling rather ruffled; she couldn't believe that moving the date of the summer fete had caused such a furore.

Gamine

impish girl or urchin (French)

First used in French to describe street urchins or playful, waif-like children, the word was incorporated into English with this meaning in the mid eighteenth century, when Thackeray used the term in *The Paris Sketchbook*. By the twentieth century its meaning had shifted and it now refers to a sexually alluring girl or woman with a slight frame, short hair and sweetly boyish or impish looks: Audrey Hepburn is often considered a classic example

Jessica kept her hat firmly on despite the warmth of the room. She had told the hairdresser she wanted to go for a gamine look, but she hadn't been prepared for a short back and sides.

Gauche

left or clumsy (French)

Anyone with even the most rudimentary grasp of French will be familiar with the word for left but 'gauche' also has another meaning: awkward or inelegant. English speakers have adopted this sense of the words but use it to describe not physical but social clumsiness. The link may be a reflection of old negative superstitions about left-handedness (we get the word 'sinister' from the Latin for left), or it may have come about as a result of the difficulties right-handers faced if when performing tasks with their left hand.

Sonya fiddled with her napkin nervously; too much fancy cutlery always made her feel gauche.

Gesundheit

health (German/Yiddish)

It's a tradition across many cultures to bless someone or wish them good health after they sneeze; Hebrew tradition has it that the soul of man was blown into Adam through his nostrils, and might leave the same way after hearty sternutation. The term is thought to have emigrated to America with the first wave of German-speaking settlers in Pennsylvania and spread more widely from 1900 onwards when large numbers of Jewish immigrants moved to the US.

James held his breath and pinched his nose, the sound of a sneeze alone was embarrassing enough in an almost silent theatre, but far worse were the cries of 'Gesundheit!' that would echo round the auditorium.

Gigolo

male escort or paid lover (French)

In the shady world of male prostitution, the gigolo is at the respectable end of the spectrum. The term is thought to come from the French '*gigolette*', which meant dancing girl or female prostitute, but in the masculine form it refers to men who are hired as either social or sexual companions for older, wealthier women. These days it describes a range of male 'service' providers, from those who receive financial support from a female lover to professional escorts who accompany women to social functions. It can also describe young men who prey upon older, wealthy women.

'I can't face going to the gala ball on my own again, Mary; I've decided it's time to hire myself a gigolo.'

Glasnost

public openness (Russian)

In 1985, Mikhail Gorbachev, leader of the former Soviet Union, introduced this word as a central tenet of his government's policy to create political transparency and allow greater freedom of speech. He hoped it would restore the Soviet Union's reputation in the world but in fact, glasnost revealed the repression and corruption that had characterized the Soviet regime and eventually led to its disintegration. The word is now used to describe any drive for openness by a government or organization.

There was to be a green glasnost at Eco-Warrior House: week one was an amnesty for unrecycled coffee cups.

Glitch

slip up (Yiddish and German)

So that's a glitch.

The exact etymology of this word is uncertain but it is believed to stem from the Yiddish word '*glitshen*' and the German '*glitschen*', both around 1962, meaning to slip or slide. It is thought to have been used for the first time in English around 1962 by American astronauts to describe a spike in voltage in an electrical current. They broadened its meaning to cover other minor technical mishaps and the rest of us have extended it still further to mean any small mishap or malfunction.

'Sorry, Simon; there's been a bit of a glitch in tonight's plans; I know it was meant to be a double date but Katie just cancelled on me. Still, three is the magic number!'

Gratis

free (Latin)

This word was incorporated into Middle English from the Latin '*gratis*', which came from '*gratiis*', meaning 'for thanks', hence without recompense. We still use it as a slang term for anything that is complementary or free of charge. Since around 1985 it has also been used in the field of computing to differentiate software that is free in the sense of not costing anything from software that is free in the sense of having freedom from legal restrictions.

'Come on, Ted; get a drink down you, we may as well make the most of it while they are gratis.'

Gravitas

heaviness, seriousness (Latin)

In Ancient Rome '*gravitas*', along with '*pietas*' (piety), '*dignitas*' (dignity) and '*iustitia*' (justice) made up the four Cardinal Virtues. It meant, as it still does today, a respectable depth of judgement and seriousness that befits a person in high office or someone in a position of responsibility. It implies the kind of moral fibre and experience that are seen as essential traits in modern day politicians (though sadly they often fall short of our expectations), or even in actors playing weighty roles.

Mr Walton sighed as the auditions drew to a close. Choosing Shakespeare for the school play had seemed such a good idea, but it was proving tricky to find a twelve-year-old with the gravitas *to play King Lear.*

Gung ho

work in harmony (Mandarin Chinese)

In Chinese the word '*gung*' translates as work, while '*ho*' means 'peace' or 'harmony'. It was an abbreviation of '*gongye hezhoushe*', the name given in the late 1930s to the industrial cooperatives springing up in rural China. It was adopted by English speakers to mean a 'can do' attitude after Lieutenant Colonel Evans Carlson of the US Marine Corps, inspired by the spirit of the cooperatives, used it as a motto for his battalion. Recently, it has developed negative associations and can mean over-enthusiastic or needlessly aggressive.

From his uncomfortable resting place in the ditch, George reflected that perhaps he'd been a little gung ho in his use of the whip for a first attempt at horse riding.

------◦◉◉◦------

Guru

teacher (Sanskrit)

Stemming from the Sanskrit root '*gru*', which means heavy or weighty, this word for teacher has its origins in Hinduism. Its connection with spiritual wisdom ensured its passage into English through the journeys of self-discovery made on the 1960s hippy trail. In the more materialistic West, its meaning expanded to include authorities on anything from footwear to designer wallpaper and, thanks to large numbers of self-styled 'gurus' with dubious qualifications, it now carries with it the faint whiff of fakery.

'Sorry, darling, I can't do tonight: I've got an appointment with my waxing guru that we both know I can't afford to miss.'

------◦◉◉◦------

Habeas corpus

you have the body (Latin)

A habeas corpus (short for '*habeas corpus ad subiiciendum*' – 'may you have the person subjected [to interrogation]') is a writ that commands a prison to bring an inmate to court so that a judge can ascertain whether they have been imprisoned lawfully or whether they should be released. Prisoners who believe they have been wrongfully detained file the writ, which must prove that the court that sentenced the prisoner made a legal or factual error if it is to be successful. The phrase stems from the medieval Latin used in the original writ, and the right of habeas corpus was later enshrined in the Habeas Corpus Act passed by Parliament in 1679.

'They've sent me down for five years, mate – I know, it's scandalous. The lawyer says he might be able to get me off though, something to do with a habeas corpus.'

Hamburger

person from Hamburg (German)

In nineteenth-century Hamburg, Germany, pounded beef patties called Hamburg steak were popular. Emigrants took it to America and 'hamburger' appeared on menus as early as 1836. By 1902 a recipe for ground beef with onion and pepper had appeared, and the modern hamburger was born. The shortening to 'burger' followed and paved the way for the cheeseburger and other variations. The freedom to enjoy a hamburger, although not formally written into the Constitution, stands side by side with the most solemn American rights of man. In Cold War Berlin, President Kennedy was said to have proclaimed himself a 'Berliner' – a kind of doughnut. There's a joke in Germany that it's lucky he wasn't in Paris ('Pariser' is old-fashioned German slang for 'condom').

'I'll have the triple-deck supreme hamburger with extra onions, extra cheese and extra bacon, a large portion of chilli fries, onion rings – and a diet Coke on the side. I'm watching my waistline.'

Hara-kiri

cutting the belly (Japanese)

In feudal Japan, Samurai warriors bound by a strict code of honour would commit suicide using 'hara-kiri' if they had shamed themselves or their masters, or if they were captured by enemies. The practice involves a ritual self-disembowelment during which the stomach is cut from side to side; the more formal term for it is '*seppuku*', though non-Samurai Japanese and Westerners have always referred to it as 'hara-kiri'. We now use the word more generically to denote figurative rather than literal acts of self-destruction.

'I'm sorry, Jasmine, but that was terrible. You simply can't pick a song that's full of notes you can't reach on a show like this – it's hara-kiri.'

Hasta la vista

see you later (Spanish)

Until 1991 this was a relatively common, though unremarkable, Spanish phrase. It made the transition into English as a kind of slang alternative to 'see you later', but wasn't used widely. Then came *Terminator 2: Judgement Day*. Arnold Schwarzenegger, playing the Terminator, said, 'Hasta la vista, baby,' every time he was about to wipe somebody out and, for reasons that remain unclear, his delivery of the line was deemed to be so witty that it was taken up by vast swathes of the English-speaking population.

'I'm sorry, Doreen. It's been lovely getting to know you but I must be off to pastures new – hasta la vista, baby.'

Haute cuisine

high cooking (French)

High quality food prepared in hierarchically run kitchens by the best chefs is known as 'haute cuisine'. Originally the phrase referred to the highest standard of French cooking, but we now apply the term to the highest standard cuisine of any origin. Official ratings such as the Michelin star system have made it easier to identify haute-cuisine restaurants, most of which place great emphasis on the presentation of their food, which has led those who prefer homelier cooking to regard the term with suspicion.

'Is there nowhere round here we can just get a steak and chips? I can't be doing with all this haute cuisine nonsense.'

Hinterland

backcountry (German)

English usage carries a resonance not present in the German usage and signifies a remote or backwoods region. Hinterland also refers to the area from which products are delivered to a port for shipping elsewhere. Historically, the term was applied to areas surrounding former European colonies in Africa, which, although not part of the colony, were influenced by the settlement, often without the safety and order which prevailed in (or was imposed upon) the colony.

The intrepid, twenty-first-century celebrities bravely essayed the hinterland with camera crew and live-links in close attendance.

Hoi polloi

the many (Greek)

In Ancient Greece, this term for the common populace had none of the negative connotations we give it today. It is thought to have passed to English via Pericles's Funeral Oration, in which he praised the democratic system in Athens for giving a voice to the many. In rather more snobbish nineteenth-century Britain, when class could be judged by whether or not you had been taught the classics, it gained its modern usage to describe the vulgar crowd, also known as the 'great unwashed'.

'Oh for goodness' sake, Jeremiah; will you please get the hoi polloi out of the VIP area.'

I think I've gone off them

Honcho
squad leader (Japanese)

It sounds like Spanish doesn't it? But in fact it comes from the Japanese word '*hancho*' that has its origins in Middle Chinese. '*Han*' translates as 'squad' and '*cho*' means 'chief', which is a common suffix in Japanese for words that denote leadership – '*kocho*', for example, means 'school principal'. The term was brought back to the US and the UK in the 1940s and 1950s by soldiers serving in Japan and Korea. English speakers use it as slang for boss, often preceded by the word 'head', which, though extraneous, does make for a pleasingly alliterative whole.

> '*OK, team, this is the beginning of a brave new era; you may think you know how to market paperclips but I'm the head honcho around here now and we'll sell them my way.*'

Hubris
insolence/pride (Greek)

In Ancient Greek society hubris was considered to be the greatest of all sins. It meant a kind of terrible pride that led to violence and caused harm to others; it was seen as a direct insult to the gods. It arrived in English in the late 1800s with its meaning only slightly watered down, to incorporate egotistical acts of vanity and exhibitions of immorality and we now use it to describe arrogance or a lack of humility particularly when it's likely to result in disaster.

'The hubris of the man astounds me – doesn't he realize that at sixty-three he's well past his horse-racing prime?'

In camera

in the chamber (Latin)

This is a legal term that means in private with a judge rather than in an open court. In general, the principal that justice must be seen to be done for it to be done at all means that courtrooms are open to reporters and the public, but there are exceptions to this rule. Cases where a witness's privacy needs to be protected, or where the disclosure of the case's details could threaten national security, can be heard in closed chambers. Photographic cameras take their name from the same source as their body is essentially a sealed box with a shutter.

'We've had some threats to the jury in this case m'lud so we'd like it to be in camera.'

In flagrante delicto

in the blazing offence (Latin)

This is a legal term that means that someone has been caught in the act of committing a crime. In modern English the phrase is often shortened to 'in flagrante' and usually preceded by the word 'caught' and so is interchangeable with 'red-handed'. Outside the law, it is used widely to refer to the interruption of any illicit act and through this usage it has also become a euphemism for being caught in a sexual act, even one where everything is above board.

The Petersons had been rather less adventurous in their love-making since they were caught in the bushes in flagrante by the vicar and his cocker spaniel.

In loco parentis

in place of a parent (Latin)

This is a legal term that relates to someone who takes responsibility for another person's child. Foster carers and legal guardians who have not adopted the child in their care are said to be *in loco parentis*. It is most commonly used in the school environment where, until the late nineteenth century, teachers shared moral responsibility for their students with the parents. It is also used in a self-referential way by parents looking after someone else's child.

'No, Daniel, you cannot have another chocolate cupcake. I'm in loco parentis *today and I know your mum wouldn't like it.'*

In vino veritas

truth in wine (Latin)

The universally acknowledged fact that alcohol loosens the tongue had been observed as far back as Ancient Rome. Pliny the Elder provided the first written reference to the phrase, describing it as a saying, so it must have been long proven even by his day. Similar sayings existed in Ancient Greek and Hebrew. In modern-day English it seems more useful than ever and it can be heard in pubs and bars across the country whenever someone breaks into a drunken rant.

Billy woke up in a cold sweat with what felt like an angry woodpecker trapped inside his head. He was entirely naked except for a small Post-it note stuck to his chest that read ominously – in vino veritas.

In vitro

in glass (Latin)

Often used in reference to laboratory experiments carried out in test tubes or other glass vessels, the term describes the artificial environment in which a test or technique is conducted outside of a living organism (an experiment which uses the complete organism is described as '*in vivo*'). The term became instantly recognized the world over after scientists conducted the first birth of a human baby from an *in vitro* fertilized human egg in 1978.

Britney never really understood in vitro *fertilization – it seemed impossible to her that a baby could have enough space to grow inside one of those narrow test tubes.*

Incognito

in disguise (Italian)

This Italian term for having your identity concealed or going by an assumed name comes from the Latin '*incognitus*', meaning 'unknown'. The term was first used in the mid seventeenth century and was widely used in wartime when spies had to assume different identities to evade discovery. It was especially used with reference to travelling without revealing your true identity, and in modern English it is often used when celebrities give false names to keep their whereabouts secret from the media.

'I'd like to check in as Mr X please – well, YOU may not recognize me, darling, but my fans are everywhere, I've simply no choice but to stay incognito.'

Incommunicado

cut off from communication (Spanish)

Most commonly used in the military, this Spanish word comes from '*incomunicar*', which means to deny communication and is used to describe a situation in which prisoners are held in seclusion with no way of contacting the outside world. In modern English use it can also refer to someone who is uncontactable due to work commitments, or is deliberately avoiding communication, either to protect their privacy or just to take a break.

'Right, if you have any questions let me know now; in half an hour's time I'm officially on holiday and I intend to be incommunicado for a full two weeks.'

Ipso facto

by the fact itself (Latin)

Frequently applied in the realms of philosophy, law and science, this term is used to assert that a particular effect is undeniably the result of the action being discussed. More commonly the term is applied to demonstrate the causal links between an action and its reaction or impact. For example, if you take out a fixed-rate mortgage, *ipso facto* you cannot benefit from changes in interest rates. The term can also be heard in settings ranging from offices to pubs by people wishing to add a flashy credence or intellectual weight to any given point.

'Look, mate: it doesn't matter what formation Chelsea play in, they've got Drogba and Anelka up front so, ipso facto, *they'll beat United.'*

Je ne sais quoi

I know not what (French)

This French phrase is always prefixed in English with 'a certain' and is used to recognize a quality or characteristic that is hard to describe, yet makes the subject in question instinctively appealing. Often used to acknowledge a woman's mystifying beauty or charisma, the phrase is also widely applied to appreciate that certain something that makes a superb plate of food so tasty or a vintage champagne so deliciously refreshing. However 'a certain *je ne sais quoi*' is increasingly being overlooked in favour of the more mundane 'X-' or 'wow factor'.

'The herbs and spices in that fillet jus just gave the whole dish a certain je ne sais quoi.'

————⁓◦◦◦⁓————

Jezebel

wicked, blasphemous woman (Hebrew)

According to Hebrew scriptures and the Old Testament, Jezebel was a queen of ancient Israel whose patronage of a pagan religion made her none too popular with the Israelites (or the prophet Elijah). She was a scheming and manipulative woman and was eventually defenestrated by her eunuchs and eaten by dogs. Though there's no evidence of it in the Bible, she has developed a reputation for sexual promiscuity and we now use Jezebel as a synonym for coquette or 'tart'.

Belinda smoothed down her skirt and hoisted her top up precisely two inches, she wanted to come across as a sophisticated seductress, not some sort of Jezebel.

————⁓◦◦◦⁓————

Jodhpurs

wide-hipped trousers, fitting tightly from knee to ankle (Anglo-Indian)

In 1459, in the heart of Rajasthan in Northern India, the ruler Rao Jodha founded the beautiful city of Jodhpur. Men of Rajasthan wore trousers of a style ideal as riding breeches, being made of a stout material with a comfortable arrangement of seams, and were thus adopted by the British during the Raj. The name 'jodhpurs' then passed into English and it is still the garment of choice for most horse-riding events and also in some military dress uniforms, although these days they are usually tight-fitting.

Although Virginia has occasionally been seen in a dress, she's happiest in jodhpurs, enjoying rides out on her pony, Tristram.

—◦◦◦—

Joie de vivre

joy of living (French)

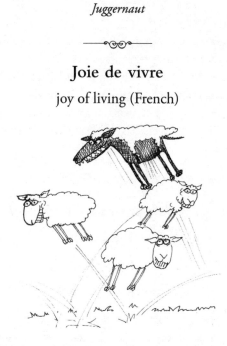

Often confused with '*joie de vie*' (joy of life), '*joie de vivre*' is in fact the even more positive attitude of the joy of living. Because of its catch-all nature the phrase can be used to express the enjoyment of specific things such as eating or drinking, or the more profound and comprehensive joy felt throughout one's whole being for the simple reality of being alive. The term is also used to describe someone who has a particularly carefree attitude.

'I don't know if it was that half a shandy I had at lunchtime, Barry, but I feel full of joie de vivre *this afternoon.'*

—◦◦◦—

Juggernaut

Lord of the Universe (Sanskrit)

Juggernaut, or Jagannatha, is one of many forms of Krishna, the revered Hindu deity, and is often represented as a young boy playing a flute. The Jagannath Temple in Puri, India is famous for its annual procession of chariots carrying statues of the deities, and British visitors who witnessed the parade in the colonial era marvelled at the 45-foot high statues, which are pushed along on sixteen wheels with diameters of seven feet. The word juggernaut has been used ever since to describe an uncontrollable force that will crush whatever falls into its path.

> *'The Juggernaut may seem a strange nickname for a man weighing only a hundred and twelve pounds, but the new flyweight champion of the world is truly unstoppable in the ring.'*

Junta

committee (Spanish)

Despite the term's origins in sixteenth-century Spanish government committees, juntas are perhaps most often associated with military dictatorships in Central or South America. A junta refers to the governing body that comes to power after a military *coup d'état*, usually formed of the heads of armed forces. However, the word is often used pejoratively today to describe governments, or senior groups within organizations, that are perceived to be dictatorial in some aspects of their policy.

> *Sir Richard was desperate to get something in writing about the extension of the hunting ban but he knew he'd have a hard time getting it past the pro-hunting junta.*

Kaftan

floor-length cotton or silk tunic (Persian)

The kaftan was an elaborately embroidered and symbolic item of clothing when it was first worn by the fourteenth-century Sultans of the Ottoman Empire; the colours, designs and trimmings denoted the status of the wearer in strictly hierarchical Ottoman society. They were also popular in Morocco, where they were traditionally a women's garment and where they were picked up by free spirits on the 1960s 'hippy trail'. The kaftan has had a fashion resurgence in the past couple of years as an item of summer beachwear.

As she tried on her twenty-sixth bikini of the day Katrina clenched her buttocks, sucked in her stomach and said a prayer of thanks for the return of the kaftan.

Kahuna

priest, expert or wizard (Hawaiian)

In Hawaiian culture, any expert in a particular art, such as boat-building, navigation or healing, was described as a 'kahuna'. Many of these ancient practices began to die out after the arrival of Christian missionaries in the 1820s, but since the 1970s some practitioners have come forward and reclaimed this ancient title. In English it is used as part of the phrase 'the big kahuna' – coined in the 1959 surfing film *Gidget* and used in the 1999 film *The Big Kahuna* starring Kevin Spacey – which means 'most important person' or 'top dog'.

'OK, who's the big kahuna here? I've got a proposition to make.'

Kamikaze

divine wind (Japanese)

The word 'kamikaze' refers to the legendary typhoon in 1281 that saved Japan from a Mongol navy assault by destroying the invader's fleet of ships. More than 660 years later the same name was given to the fearless World War II Japanese fighter pilots who loaded their planes with explosives and deliberately crashed into enemy targets. In 1941 kamikaze pilots destroyed four US Navy battleships during the invasion of Pearl Harbor. Today the term is frequently used both seriously and more light-heartedly to describe behaviour or actions so reckless as to be suicidal.

High on drugs, with police in hot pursuit, the car-jacker was on a kamikaze mission through the busy streets.

This is the catering corps, isn't it?

Kaput

broken (German)

The German word '*kaputt*' means lost, ruined or broken but it comes from the comparatively undramatic French phrase '*être capot*', which means to score zero at a round of cards and the Germans picked it up as a term for being defeated or ruined. In English, where it began to be used in the late nineteenth century, it usually refers to objects that are broken. The explosion of the Vanguard TV3 rocket shortly after launch in 1957 led the press to dub it 'Kaputnik'.

There was no way Owen could salvage his turbo hairdryer now: it went completely kaput when he tried to give his dog a blow-dry.

Karaoke

empty orchestra (Japanese)

'*Kara*' in Japanese means empty and '*okesutora*' means 'orchestra'. Japanese drummer Daisuke Inoue was often asked by guests in the coffee shops where he played to provide an instrumental recording of his performance so that they could sing along in their own homes. Inoue saw a gap in the market and manufactured a machine that would play his backing tracks for 100 yen per song. He then leased his karaoke machines out to restaurants and hotels and the craze for amateur performances of popular songs took off, soon finding a much-loved place in British bars and pubs.

Somehow Joseph's karaoke performances improved as the night wore on, and by midnight he could sing both Elton John's and George Michael's parts in 'Don't Let the Sun Go Down on Me'.

Karma

act, action, performance (Sanskrit)

Karma is the idea that one's actions actively influence one's future in a cycle of cause and effect. Originating in Ancient India, the concept is a key feature of many philosophies and generally asserts that an individual's own actions influence their future happiness. Today the idea is framed more by notions of an action bringing good or bad luck than by spiritual goodness.

'OK, five more minutes of bitching and then we stop – it's bad karma.'

Kayak

hunter's boat (Inuit)

The Inuits used small one-person paddleboats for hunting in the icy sub-Arctic waters and it is thought that the word was imported into European languages by Dutch or Danish whalers and then made its way into English by the early eighteenth century. Though no longer made from animal skins, the modern version of the boat is very like the original in shape and is popular with white-water adrenaline-seekers who like to bob about in the rapids in just a thin plastic shell.

'I'm just not ready for a relationship at the moment,' Tina told Ralph at the end of the night. It seemed kinder than telling him she'd rather row a kayak over Niagara Falls than endure his halitosis for a moment longer.

Kebab

marinated meat cooked on a skewer (Arabic)

The Arabic word '*kabab*' is possibly derived through ancient Semitic languages from '*kabābu*' meaning 'to burn or char'. '*Döner kebab*', in Turkish, literally means 'rotating meat'. '*Shish*' means skewer, hence '*shish kebab*'. One modern version was invented by Mahmut Aygün (1921–2009), known as the kebab king, who opened a Turkish restaurant in Berlin serving traditional sliced lamb in warm pitta bread instead of on a plate. However, he failed to patent his invention . . . The ancient institution of the British pub and the ancient traditions of delicious Middle Eastern cuisine combine so well they're now an indispensable part of British culture.

When the landlord called time and Terry suggested a kebab, Julie realized they would be together always.

Ketchup

fish brine (Malay, from '*kichap*')

Yes, Heinz's most popular condiment began life as a spicy pickled fish sauce in seventeenth-century China. The word is a Westernized version of the Malay word '*kichap*', which came from the Min Chinese '*koechiap*', meaning 'fish brine'. The sweet red version we're familiar with began to take shape when American seamen added tomatoes – excellent for preventing scurvy. In 1876 John Heinz launched his tomato ketchup and it's been a staple of British and American diets ever since.

'Thanks so much for agreeing to look after him, Sarah. Here's his toothbrush and his nightclothes, oh, and his bottle of ketchup – he won't eat anything without it.'

Khaki

dusty (Hindi)

Until the early nineteenth century the uniform of the British Army featured bright scarlet tunics; a useful means of identifying who was on your side in the confusion of the battlefield. However it also made solders highly visible targets for ambushes and enemy snipers, and heavy casualties in colonial wars led to the introduction of the dun-coloured uniforms still worn by soldiers today. The word comes from the Hindi for dust or earth, with which the troops blended well in their new attire, and can be used to describe the fabric of the uniforms as well as the colour.

Neville smoothed down his hair and turned to look in the mirror. He'd always fancied himself as a young Alec Guinness and, in his new khaki shirt, he felt sure he looked just like him.

Kiosk

pavilion, palace (Turkish)

The telephone kiosk sounds like a quintessentially British invention, but the word itself has far more exotic origins. In seventeenth-century Turkey they were porticoed palaces grand enough to attract the attention of Lady Wortley Montagu, wife of the English ambassador to Istanbul, who wrote a letter home about them. In modern English, however, they tend to refer to somewhat less genteel mobile stands selling hot drinks or cheap goods on the street or in shopping malls.

'I can't possibly drink this coffee, Muriel. You may as well confess now – you got it from that kiosk on the corner, didn't you?'

Kitsch

tat, gaudy merchandise (German)

Language experts believe that this word is derived from the German verb '*kitschen*', which meant 'to scrape mud from the street'. It is believed to have become associated with garish, shoddily produced artwork in late nineteenth-century Munich, where cheap, gaudy paintings that appealed to the uncultivated tastes of the newly wealthy Munich middle classes were hot produce. The word signified socially aspirational poor taste, though in the past decade 'kitsch' has become fashionable (in a postmodern, ironic sort of way, of course).

> *'How much for that red and gold version of the* Mona Lisa? *It's so kitsch I just have to have it.'*

Klutz

blockhead (Yiddish)

This comes from the Yiddish word '*klots*', which translates literally as wooden beam, and perhaps also from the German word '*klotz*', meaning block or lump. '*Klotz*' is related to the English words 'clot' and 'clod', both of which mean lump (of earth in the latter case) and also stupid person.

The president blushed as he walked head on into the glass swing door. He liked his reputation as a man of the people, but he didn't want anyone thinking he was a klutz.

⸺◦⟨⟩◦⸺

Kohl

black powder (Arabic)

Kohl is the name for the dark grey or black powdered mineral that has been used in the Middle East since the Bronze Age, when it amplified the beauty of Egyptian queens and was also used as a protection from eye infections due to its antibacterial properties. It is still used in its original form in South Asia, where it is often put around the eyes of infants to protect them from the evil eye. We now use the word to describe heavily applied chemical-based eyeliner.

Kirsty staggered to the bathroom and braved the mirror – her hair stood on end as if she'd been electrocuted and last night's sexy, kohl-ringed eyes now made her look like a despondent panda.

⸺◦⟨⟩◦⸺

Kosher

suitable and pure (Yiddish)

Food that has been prepared according to Jewish dietary rituals and laws is deemed 'kosher', or fit to eat. It came from the Hebrew word '*kasher*', meaning fit and lawful, around 1851, but since the end of the nineteenth century the word has been used more generically outside the Jewish community to mean 'legitimate'. It is still commonly used with this meaning, especially in the East End of London, where cockneys use it to indicate that something is all above board.

'Do you want to come in with me on this horse then, Stan? It's kosher, I promise you.'

Kowtow

knock the head (Chinese)

The most deeply respectful act of submission in Han Chinese culture was the 'kowtow'. The word describes a kneeling bow so deep that the forehead touches the ground. By the 1820s the word had come to mean an obsequious manner of acting, and it is in this sense that the word has been adopted into English. In the less strictly hierarchical West the term is usually used in a negative sense, to describe the actions of someone who is grovelling or 'sucking up' to their superiors.

Mark Stainton dressed with care on the morning of his interview. He had no intention of kowtowing to the new manager, but he hoped that a clean shirt and tie would create the right impression.

Kudos

glory, renown (Greek)

'Kudos' is a singular noun in Greek and it entered British English in this form at the end of the eighteenth century, but in America the final 's' is mistakenly thought to mean the word is plural, so the word 'kudo' has been adopted as a singular. 'Kudos' is found in American English, but only when someone has received more than one accolade. Both spellings are used to denote public respect or acclaim.

By the final leg of the squadron's assault course Melanie could barely breathe, let alone run. But she wouldn't give up; she wanted the kudos of being the first female officer to finish before the Sergeant Major.

Sudoku champion of Athens ten years ago, and he never lets you forget it.

Lacrosse

game of hooked sticks (French Canadian)

Lacrosse was originally a Native American team game played using curved sticks to scoop and throw the ball and was adopted by French Canadians in the early eighteenth century. They named the game '*jeu de la crosse*', literally meaning 'game of the hooked stick' and an abbreviated version of the phrase – lacrosse – found its way into North American English. It is now particularly popular in girls' schools where the hooked end of the sticks inflicts serious damage to bony shins.

> *'OK, girls, today we're going to have a mini lacrosse tournament, but let's keep it clean, shall we? We don't want a repeat of "Bloody Thursday".'*

Lager

storehouse (German)

The term is short for '*Lagerbier*' – a '*Lager*' being the storehouse or cellar in which beer ferments. A vast range of flavours and degrees of dryness exist in Germany, less so elsewhere. In certain regions, like Bavaria, lager is central to traditional culture. Lager is the drink of choice for many youngsters in Britain, including a rowdy subset called 'lager-louts'. Older people tend to prefer bitter, less fizzy native beers at cellar temperature (the American notion of warm English beer is a misconception). Lager is best enjoyed cold and in the US may be served in a frosted mug.

> *Roy's philosophy was mellower, and Melissa prettier, after six pints of lager.*

Laissez-faire

let do, leave alone (French)

'Laissez-faire' typically describes an economic or political philosophy that promotes a reduction of government intervention in aspects of society, particularly business and industry. The phrase's first recorded use was by French Minister René de Voyer in his famous outburst, '*Laissez faire, morbleu! Laissez faire!*' ('Leave them be, damn it! Leave them be!') Today the term is used to describe non-interventionist approaches in other settings, such as schools with liberal discipline policies. More generally it is used to describe an individual with a laid-back, or even lazy attitude.

'This is the last straw, Mr Streathers. The students are running riot, one of them is hot-wiring a teacher's car as we speak. The time for a laissez-faire approach is well and truly over.'

Lebensraum

living space (German)

This comes from the German words '*Leben*', meaning 'life' and '*Raum*' meaning 'space', but its meaning is more complex than it seems. '*Lebensraum*' was the living space that Hitler decided the German people needed to become a truly great race, and it was to acquire this extra space that he invaded his neighbouring countries to the east. The term was first used in this sense in 1897 by geographer and ethnographer Friedrich Ratzel, who studied the English and French colonies and thought Germany should have its own. It is usually used today to describe territory that is being fought over.

Sidney looked around his dingy room in despair. In his dreams of the city he'd been living in luxury, not competing for Lebensraum *with a swarm of cockroaches.*

Leitmotif

leading theme (German)

This is a musical theme that recurs whenever the composer wants the idea of a certain character, place or concept to come across. The word stems from '*leiten*', 'to lead', and '*Motif*', meaning 'theme'. The first use of the term dates back to the late 1800s when it was used exclusively in reference to music and became associated with Wagner's epic operas. It is still used in reference to classical music as well as for modern compositions and film scores. It has also expanded to include recurrent themes in other creative works, such as poetry, dance, painting and fiction.

The sea was wonderfully warm, but Kerry could only paddle. As soon as the water reached her knees the shark's leitmotif from Jaws *boomed inside her head and made her run for dry land.*

Lingua franca
Frankish language (Italian)

In the medieval Middle East, Europeans were collectively known by Arabic speakers as Franks and the Frankish language was primarily Italian with a mixture of Persian, French, Greek and Arabic words. It was a language cobbled together to allow people of different native tongues to communicate. We now use the term to refer to any common language used by speakers of different languages, especially where that language is not the native tongue of either. English, for instance, has become the lingua franca of the international business world.

'Have you ever tried taking minutes of a meeting where half the delegates are Chinese and the other half Icelandic? I'm just praying English is the lingua franca.'

Loot
plunder (Anglo-Indian, from the Hindi '*lut*')

'Loot' or '*lut*' originally described the items stolen following a war or riot and was brought into the English language by British soldiers who served in India in the late eighteenth century. Over time it has also become a verb and 'looting' is often reported in war-torn towns. We also use the word more casually as slang for money or a particularly pleasing haul of presents.

Hermione loved birthdays. Before bed she arranged her gifts in rows on her bedroom floor and surveyed her loot with glee.

That is looting – this is connoisseurship.

❦

Louche

decadent, shady (French)

This comes from the Old French word '*lousche*', which means 'squint-eyed'. A squint was clearly a suspicious affliction in those days because the term gave rise to the more modern 'louche' meaning devious and of questionable repute. The word was first used in English in the early nineteenth century and can be used in reference to a person of dubious moral values, or their debauched behaviour. It is also often used to describe a decadent or possibly slightly seedy place.

'It's very tricky to know what sort of place you're going into in that part of town, some of the bars look terribly louche.'

Macho

virile, domineering (Spanish)

In Spanish culture (and in Hollywood), the macho man is celebrated as a strong, patriarchal, responsible example of the alpha male. The word comes from 'machismo', which has also been adopted by English speakers and means 'masculinity'. It has been used in English since the 1920s but in Britain and America (apart from in the movies) it is most often used negatively to denote aggression, chauvinism or the kind of yobbish physical posturing that starts fights after last orders.

'Don't you dare go all macho on me, Darren; you're no Sylvester Stallone, and anyway, you know I prefer a man who's in touch with his feminine side.'

Maestro

master, teacher (Italian)

This, like so many musical words, is Italian and usually refers to composers, conductors and some musicians of classical music and opera. It has its origins in the Latin *'magister'*, meaning 'master', and in modern usage it has expanded to include masters in other artistic fields, particularly fine art, and some sports, such as fencing, where it means instructor, though its principal use is still in the musical world.

With a final frantic wave of his baton and a wild flick of his hair, the maestro brought the opera to its magnificent conclusion.

Magnum opus

great work (Latin)

This grand term refers to the largest or most substantial piece of work by an established composer, author or artist. These days we tend to use the phrase as a synonym for masterpiece, and in many cases both terms apply, but a magnum opus is not always an artist's best work. It might refer to a piece of work that is remarkable more for its scale, or the time it took to produce, than its success.

Lucille scanned the desk in front of her: seven lined notepads, fifteen biros and a box of twenty-four Krispy Kreme doughnuts. Yes, she had everything she needed to begin her magnum opus.

Mañana

tomorrow (Spanish)

This comes from the Latin '*maneana*', which translates as 'early tomorrow', but to the Spanish, and to most English-speaking users of the phrase, it means at an unspecified time the next day. Though it is used straightforwardly in Spain, in English it has taken on an additional sense of vagueness or reluctance to commit to a deadline. We sometimes say that someone has a *mañana* attitude, which means they're so laid-back that they never get anything done.

'*All you ever tell me is,* mañana, mañana! *Well I'm sick of hearing it – we both know* mañana *never comes.*'

Mandarin

official (Malay)

The name given to sixteenth-century Chinese officials is derived from the Malay word '*mantri*', meaning 'minister of state'. English speakers have adopted the term to describe government officials of our own, and also for the small, sweet citrus fruit, so named because its colour is the same shade as the Chinese mandarins' robes. In their honour, the word is also put to use as a name for society's elite, such as influential figures in the art world.

'*Personally, I don't think that a banana placed on top of a toilet cistern constitutes art, whether the mandarins in charge of the Turner Prize will agree remains to be seen.*'

Mantra

instrument of thought (Sanskrit)

This comes from the Sanskrit root '*man*', meaning 'to think', and the suffix '*tra*', meaning 'tool'. If refers to a chant or sound, made either out loud or in the mind, that advances spiritual development. They have found their way into English through the teachings of Buddhism and Hinduism, though we now use the word in a more secular sense. Any saying or statement that helps us to focus on achieving something can be labelled a mantra.

'I've borrowed my New Year's resolution from a sportswear company: just do it! I'm going to make that my mantra.'

Maven

expert (Yiddish)

Maven comes from the Yiddish word '*meyvn*', which stems from the Hebrew word '*binah*', meaning understanding. It traditionally referred to someone who gathers information and passes their knowledge on to others. It arrived in English in the 1950s and was popularized in the 1960s Vita herring adverts, which featured 'The Beloved Herring Maven'. Sociologist Malcolm Gladwell uses it in his best-selling book *The Tipping Point* to describe intense information gatherers who are quick to pick up new trends. We also use it to describe someone who is an authority on a subject.

Douglas had a job he loved – selling fishing bait. In fact, he was so skilled at breeding worms for the wire that the angling community nicknamed him the 'Maggot Maven'.

Mazel tov

good fortune (Yiddish)

With its origins in the Mishnaic Hebrew word '*mazzal*', meaning destiny, this word is used to celebrate good fortune having come someone's way. It is traditionally used on significant occasions such as weddings and bar mitzvahs, though it is also now widely used even outside the Jewish community as an alternative to congratulations for anything from buying a new house to passing your exams.

> *'Hi, Louise, guess what? It was third time lucky with my driving test – I've passed!'*
>
> *'That's brilliant! Right – stay where you are, I'm coming straight round to say* mazel tov.*'*

Mea culpa

my fault (Latin)

This phrase comes from a Roman Catholic prayer for Mass called '*Confiteor*', meaning 'I confess', which includes the cheery line: 'I have sinned exceedingly in thought, word and deed: through my fault, through my own fault.' This English translation appeared beside the Latin in prayer books and the phrase was absorbed into general use. Now, a mea culpa is an admission of guilt for a mistake, often rendered as 'mea maxima culpa' by people into serious breast-beating.

> *Someone among us has left their underwear in the microwave where I can only assume they were attempting to dry it. I suggest they perform a swift mea culpa if they want the chance to salvage the offending item.*

Memento mori

be mindful of death (Latin)

Something ... something... where is thy sting?

In Ancient Rome, where life could, though disease or war, be brutally short, this phrase was used as a reminder of mortality. It is said to have been delivered by an appointed slave to victorious generals after a celebration of victory to help them guard against complacency. Under the influence of Christianity the phrase came to refer to works of art: paintings, elegies and engravings on tombs were common versions.

> *'Don't be too hard on the boy about those plastic skulls he likes to dangle off his ears, Pete. Try to think of them as religious ornamentation – they're the perfect memento mori.'*

Ménage à trois

household of three (French)

In the affair-fuelled society of late nineteenth-century England this French term for a domestic arrangement in which three people live together and have a sexual relationship came in rather handy for the British aristocracy. Any household in which a married couple live with the lover of one partner can be described with this word. It is sometimes used in modern times to refer to the act of sex between three people, more colloquially known as a 'threesome'.

> *'I wouldn't mind a* ménage à trois *if I'm honest, it'd get him off my case every night and it'd be nice to share the housework.'*

Mi casa es su casa

my house is your house (Spanish)

This welcoming Spanish phrase is used widely in Spanish and Mexican households to make guests feel at home. It passed into

American English through the Latin American and Spanish communities and subsequently reached British shores. While it can be used quite formally by Spanish speakers, it is more of a light-hearted phrase in English, where people tend to say it with arms thrown theatrically wide.

> *'Friends, come on in – no, no need to take off your shoes James,* mi casa es su casa, *let me get you a drink.'*

Mise en scène

staging, direction (French)

This term is central to the critical analysis of film and theatre and refers to everything that can be seen in the picture or onstage: the set, costumes, lighting and the use of movement and expression by the actors. It was first used by critics in the French film journal *Les Cahiers du cinéma* in the 1950s and is still central to the vocabulary of film and drama critics today.

> *Walter Jackman wasn't happy, he sat in the director's chair but the damned actors seemed to be running the show. And what did any of them know about the* mise en scène?

Modus operandi

mode of operation (Latin)

This started as a term used by the police to describe the favoured methods of criminals. In cases where a series of crimes had been committed the investigating team would try to establish the criminal's characteristic techniques and patterns of movement to plan their capture. It is still used in this way today (often shortened to MO) though it is most often applied generally to a person's method of working that has proved successful.

> *'Good lord, Gwynneth; seven children to ferry to ballet class, football club, Mandarin for beginners and orienteering practice, and you still have to squeeze in the shopping for dinner. Tell me how you manage it – what's your modus operandi?'*

Moratorium

delay (Latin)

In law a 'moratorium' is an officially authorized period of delay in complying with a legal demand, such as payment of a debt, or a legally enforced suspension of an activity while discussions take place concerning its future. Since its introduction into English in around 1875, there have been moratoria on activities as diverse as hunting, mining, nuclear testing and the death penalty. In more general modern use it means a pause or break from something.

> *'Can we please have a moratorium on these awful round-robin joke emails? They're blocking up my inbox and they're not even funny.'*

Nabob

wealthy man/dignitary (Hindi)

During the Mogul Empire, a governor in India was known as a *'nawab'*, or 'nabob', which comes from the Arabic *'na'ib'*, meaning deputy. The riches they took home after their time in the East marked them out as wealthy men and the term 'nabob' was coined to describe a man with immense riches, especially one who had made his fortune in the Orient. It is now used as an alternative to 'bigwig' to denote someone in a position of influence who has power and wealth.

Janet smoothed the crumples out of her jacket and stepped closer to the VIP bar; she wasn't used to mingling with nabobs and felt in need of a stiff gin and tonic.

NB (Nota Bene)

note well (Latin)

This useful Latin phrase is usually abbreviated to NB and means 'note well' in the sense of 'pay attention'. Though used in conversation in Roman times, the phrase is reserved for text in modern English, where it is used to draw attention to a particularly important fact that is linked in some way to the primary reading material. It is most commonly used by teachers who wish to highlight information that their students need to take into account.

Sophie's note taking had never been sophisticated. Usually she got down the gist of what the teacher said and then put NBs in the margins whenever she realized she'd missed something important.

Nil desperandum

nothing to be despaired at (Latin)

Like so many of our best maxims this comes from Roman lyric poet Horace, who wrote it in *Odes I*, published in 23 BC. 'Nil' comes from '*nihil*', meaning 'nothing', and '*desperandum*' meaning 'to be despaired at'. It was probably adopted into English as a salve to the soul in difficult times and we still use the phrase when we need to cheer someone up as an alternative to 'it's not the end of the world'.

> '*Nil desperandum, William; there's no shame in playing on the B team, my boy.*'

Actually, old chap, it's not helping much.

Noblesse oblige

nobility obligates (French)

This term sums up the idea that those of high birth have an obligation towards the rest of society. Originally it implied that noblemen owed it to themselves and to others to become strong leaders of common men, though over time it has become less explicit. Nowadays it is used to suggest that those with wealth and status should do something to help those less fortunate than themselves.

'I do like Prince Charles, you know. I don't know if it's noblesse oblige *but he really does seem to do a lot of good with his charity work.'*

Nom de plume

pen name (French)

Though the phrase is French, it is rarely used in France, where *'nom de guerre'*, meaning 'war name', has served as an alternative to 'pseudonym' since the establishment of the French Resistance. The phrase 'nom de plume' was in fact made up by the English, who wanted a literary-sounding phrase for writers wishing to disguise their identity. They were especially useful to female writers in the male-dominated world of publishing, Mary Ann Evans famously wrote under the name George Eliot to ensure that her work was taken seriously.

'What do you think of Crumpet Delamore as my nom de plume? I think it has the perfect ring of romance for an author of a Mills & Boon.'

Non sequitur

does not follow (Latin)

This term refers to a statement or response that seems utterly meaningless in the context of whatever preceded it. It came into English around 1540 and when a non sequitur is used deliberately, it is usually the preserve of comedians who aim to make a comment so ludicrously absurd and irrelevant that it becomes funny. It may also be used in an argument when someone wants to outwit their opponent by confusing them with nonsense.

'I think I'll have cake, but should it be plum or Victoria sponge?'
'Don't try and evade me with your non sequiturs. Did you scoop up the doggy doos or not?'

Nosh

snack food (Yiddish)

This beautifully onomatopoeic word comes from another Yiddish word '*nashn*', which means 'to eat sweets', or 'to nibble on'. It was adopted into English by the working-class communities in the East End of London, where there was a large Jewish population in the early 1900s. It has become a slang word for food and is often preceded by the word 'posh' to refer to cooking that is considered fancy.

'Alright darlin', how's about we head up West tonight and I'll treat you to a nice bit of nosh.'

———∘⟨⟨⟩⟩∘———

Nous

mind, intellect (Greek)

To Homer it meant 'mental activity', to Plato it denoted the conscious part of the soul, while for Aristotle it represented the intellect. However, in spite of these varying interpretations, 'nous' was generally accepted as a philosophical term for the mind. It continued to be used in this way by later philosophers but in modern English it has far less cerebral connotations and is used simply to mean 'common sense'.

> *'That hairdresser could make a fortune out of all the secrets she knows about the rich and famous but she just doesn't have the nous – that's why they all like her.'*

———∘⟨⟨⟩⟩∘———

Nouveau riche

new rich (French)

Trade and economic growth have led to shifting fortunes between the social classes since the earliest civilizations, but during the Industrial Revolution the British borrowed the French term for those with newly acquired wealth who were breaking into aristocratic social circles for the first time. It was used as it is today; as a derogatory term, laden with the suggestion that, as the beneficiaries of new money rather than old, the 'nouveau riche' would lack the taste and breeding to know how to use their wealth wisely and discreetly.

> *'I'm sorry darling, but we really can't go for dinner with the new neighbours; those big china bulldogs in their driveway are so painfully nouveau riche.'*

Nul points

no points (French)

The catchphrase of the Eurovision Song Contest was first made famous in the competition's 1962 show, when Belgian crooner Fud Leclerc was awarded a tragic '*nul points*' for his rendition of pop ballad 'Ton Nom'. It seemed funny to the English-speaking audience to hear 'no points' read out in every European language, and the phrase entered the English lexicon as a marker of any truly dire performance.

'I'm going to really cause some pain at the karaoke club tonight lads, you watch – they don't call me "Nul Points Nichols" for nothing.'

Oeuvre

work (French)

The French use this word to mean work in the sense of an artist's work, rather than the daily grind, and '*oeuvre*' usually refers to the complete body of work by a writer, artist or composer. It entered English in 1875, and is used primarily in artistic criticism or by academics who are looking at the life's work of an individual to assess it in its widest possible context. It is generally viewed as a rather pretentious word, though it has seen resurgence through use by modern music reviewers.

Henry had studied the entire Bee Gees oeuvre but he still couldn't fathom how Barry hit those high notes.

Ombudsman

commission man (Swedish)

This word can be traced back to the Danish law of Jutland in 1241. It was then written as '*umbozman*' and meant royal civil servant. By 1809 the term was established with its modern meaning of 'official' with the creation of the Swedish Parliamentary Ombudsman to protect the rights of its citizens. In England the word is most often used to describe Parliamentary officials, though they can work for a range of organizations in the public interest.

'How dare they give me a speeding fine when I was doing twenty-six miles per hour in a twenty-five-mile per hour zone! I'm telling you, Penelope, there should be an ombudsman to deal with this kind of injustice.'

Outré

exaggerated, eccentric (French)

Used in English since around 1720, this French word is derived from '*outre*', meaning 'beyond', and originally described any behaviour, design or action that broke the boundaries of eighteenth-century convention. It is now regularly used in reference to extravagant fashions, where it might be taken as a compliment by an innovative designer, or to outlandish interior decoration, where it would probably be taken as an insult.

> *'I don't think I'd go back there again would you, Gordon?*
> *The food was delicious, but the faux tiger-skin rugs and zebra*
> *hide chairs seemed rather outré for a family restaurant.'*

Panache

plume (French)

There's always someone who has to go over the top.

The literal translation refers to the feather worn in the helmet of King Henri IV of France, whose bravery and flamboyance gave the word its idiomatic meaning. It describes an almost reckless heroism best exemplified by French dramatist Edmond Rostand's most famous character, Cyrano de Bergerac (created in 1897), who admired King Henri's courage and was partly responsible for establishing 'panache' as a desirable quality in a person. We now also use it in reference to anything that exudes flair, from a musical performance to an outstandingly cooked meal.

'There are some who say The Boulder's wrestling days are over, but he delivered that pumphandle slam with real panache.'

Paparazzi

mosquitos (Italian)

This word is now used across the world for freelance photographers who pursue celebrities to take candid shots of them, but it didn't acquire this meaning until the 1966 release of Federico Fellini's *La Dolce Vita*. Fellini had based one of the film's characters on a street photographer called Tazio Secchiaroli, who made his name with surreptitiously taken images of famous people having angry outbursts or arguments. He supposedly named the character Signore Paparazzo, after a school friend whose buzzing energy had earned him the nickname 'The Mosquito'.

Tamara never used the front entrance to department stores; the paparazzi made window shopping impossible.

Par excellence

pre-eminent (French)

The very best thing of its kind or the most skilled person in their field is referred to with this phrase. Its literal and original meaning – to a degree of excellence – has been largely superseded by a still more effusive one: the most excellent of all. Exactly when and why it was adopted into English is unclear, especially since our own word 'pre-eminent' does the job equally well, but the French flourish adds a certain distinguished flair.

Lord Hurlington spent most of his days reminiscing about his time in the armed forces; in his day, he'd been hailed as a military tactician par excellence, but was now reduced to waging war on the moles in his back garden.

Pariah

untouchable, social outcast (Anglo-Indian)

The original pariahs, or 'Pariars' are a Tamil tribe of drummers named after the Pari drum. After the introduction of the Indian caste system in around 1500 BC they were segregated from the Hindu majority and are discriminated against as 'untouchables' who are outside the caste system – literally outcasts. British colonialists witnessed the exclusion and social rejection of the Pariahs and from 1819 used their name to describe all those who are spurned by society.

Councillor Waterford was beginning to regret his decision to support plans for a new giant supermarket in the district. He had become a pariah in the village and even the milkman had stopped calling at his house.

Passé

past (French)

It is fitting that a country where being in fashion is a matter of national pride should have provided us with a neat little word to indicate when something is looking a bit jaded. We use this word as the French do, in the sense of 'past it', to indicate something that is no longer, ahem, à la mode (see p.10). It can be applied to artistic, culinary and musical styles as well as to clothing, and is most frequently used by those who believe their own tastes to be unimpeachable.

'No, Nigel, there's nothing that will work for me here; ivory makes me look washed out and floaty chiffon is so passé.'

Look, sabre-tooth tiger teeth! How Middle Palaeolithic is that?

Passim

throughout, everywhere (Latin)

This is a rather bookish word that has been passed on to us by Ancient Roman scholars. It is used in footnotes, indexes or other explanatory material to show that an idea or particular word is referred to repeatedly at various points in the work being cited. It comes from the Latin word '*passus*', which is the past participle of '*pandere*', meaning 'to spread', and allows references to be made to a text as a whole rather than pinpointing precise passages.

New evidence suggested that evolution was dependent on a process of natural selection (Darwin, On the Origin of Species, *1859,* passim*).*

Peccadillo

small sin (Spanish)

This word came to us in the late sixteenth century from the Spanish, who got their word from the Latin '*peccare*', meaning to sin. But it refers only to the mildest of transgressions; an individual's bad habits are often described as their 'peccadillos', as long as they are mildly annoying rather than seriously antisocial, and a one-off trivial misdeed might also be described as such.

At the start of their relationship Jean had been charmed by Alfred's little peccadillos, but as she swept his toenail trimmings off the edge of the bathtub for the hundredth time, she knew she had to say goodbye.

Per se

by, of itself (Latin)

Another Latin term useful in argument, 'per se' means by virtue of itself; 'per' is Latin for 'by' or 'through', and 'se' means 'itself.' It is used in law as part of the phrase 'illegal per se', which is used to refer to something that is against the law in its own right, and also in general argument in place of the word necessarily.

Melanie wasn't averse to fancy dress per se, but in her opinion attempting to look like a playboy bunny after the age of forty was taking things too far.

—◦◦◦◦—

Persona non grata

unwelcome person (Latin)

This phrase has endured in the English language primarily through its usefulness in diplomatic circles. It refers to a member of diplomatic staff who is deemed to be no longer welcome in a country, either because they are suspected of being a spy or there has been a breakdown of trust between the two nations. The phrase has taken on a broader meaning in general use and is applied to people who have been cut off or ostracized from a group.

> *Eddie had stopped attending the Poetry Society's live perform-ance nights; he felt he'd been made* persona non grata *when he admitted to not having read* Beowulf *in the original Old English.*

—◦◦◦◦—

Pied-à-terre

foot on the ground (French)

A small city apartment that serves as a temporary home during the working week is known as a 'pied-à-terre'. The literal transla-tion of the phrase gives a sense of its purpose as a foothold in a metropolis. They are usually second homes, with the owner's primary property being larger and in a more rural setting, and so the phrase has a certain sense of luxury.

> *'Oh, Donald, I'm sick of this long journey home every time we go out in town. Can't we get ourselves a sweet little pied-à-terre like Clive and Susan's?'*

Placebo

I shall please (Latin)

In the seventeenth century, a 'placebo' was a treatment given by a doctor purely to please a patient. Later, with the advent of clinical trials, the word was adopted to describe the mock medication given to some patients in the control experiment, in order to ensure that the changes being observed in the main experiment are the result of the drug being tested, rather than the patient's belief in the medication. We now also use the term 'placebo effect' to describe any positive outcome that is caused by a belief in something's effectiveness.

> *'Those tablets definitely did something for me doctor, I don't know if it was just the placebo effect but the minute I got home from the chemist I've been like clockwork.'*

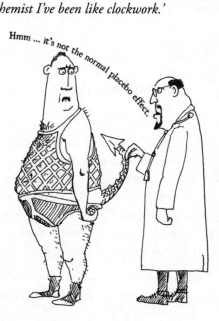

—◦◦◦—

Poltergeist

noisy ghost (German)

Distinct from apparitions that materialize, poltergeists remain unseen but make noises and perpetrate acts of mischief such as throwing objects around. In German, '*poltern*' means 'to make noise' and '*Geist*' means 'ghost'. Sceptics say poltergeist activity that can't be dismissed as fraud has physical explanations such as static electricity, electromagnetic fields or infrasound. However, some well-documented cases with reliable witnesses are hard to explain. Traditionally, poltergeist activity may occur around disturbed or hysterical individuals.

> *Stephan went to sleep each night that week hoping he'd wake up with the Norovirus:* Poltergeist *was his favourite horror film of all time and he wanted to experience projectile vomiting for himself.*

—◦◦◦—

Post-mortem

after death (Latin)

A post-mortem is the examination of a body after death. They have been carried out for more than two thousand years; one of the earliest was performed on Julius Caesar in 44 BC and by the early twentieth century they had become standard practice for any death where the cause was uncertain. We still use the term to describe this procedure, though it is also commonly used to describe any review or analysis that takes place after the completion of an event.

> *'OK, lads, I think we all know we could have played better, but there's no need for a big post-mortem – let's just focus on the games we've still got ahead of us.'*

Prêt-à-porter

ready-to-wear (French)

High-end fashion designers used to make all their clothes on a personal basis for their individual, high-paying clients, but by the mid 1950s there was a widespread desire for designer clothes at more accessible prices. Prêt-à-porter or ready-to-wear collections were the answer to this, allowing greater access to skilfully designed but mass-produced clothes. Many designers still make made-to-measure outfits for their most loyal clients, but the vast majority now focus on their prêt-à-porter range.

'It is gorgeous, Felipe, but you know I can't go in prêt-à-porter – I'd never live it down if someone else was wearing the same thing as me.'

Prima donna

first lady (Italian)

Yeah, she hates yellow flowers.

This term was coined in Italian opera houses to describe the leading female singer in the company, usually a soprano, who, according to opera mythology, was self-important, demanding and egotistical. The phrase is now more commonly used to describe self-obsessed female stars with a reputation for a bad temper and an outrageously long list of dressing room requirements, such as freshly painted white walls, rare Guatemalan orchids and full kitchen facilities for their personal chef.

'I'm telling you, Yvonne, I've done hair and make-up for some of the biggest stars out there, but that little one-hit wonder is the biggest prima donna I've ever come across.'

Pro bono

for good (Latin)

This is a shortened version of the phrase '*pro bono publico*', which means 'for public good'. It refers to the work that lawyers do without payment for clients who are unable to pay their fees or for charities or non-profit-making organizations. In recent years it has also been used to describe the ethos of public service organizations, like the National Health Service and the BBC, which are run to provide a service rather than to make a profit.

'I'm leaving the law firm. I've got so much pro bono work I'm going to set up a charity instead.'

Protégé

protected person, apprentice (French)

A person being mentored or guided in their profession by someone more experienced is known as a 'protégé'. The word, which entered English in 1778, comes from the French '*proteger*' meaning 'to protect' and was originally used in relation to someone apprenticed to an established tradesman in order to learn their skills. These days it is often used in a looser sense to refer to someone who is favoured, though not necessarily trained, by an expert in their field.

'Colin, I believe that you have great potential, the world of bathroom and kitchen tile grouting needs someone like you – I'm going to make you my protégé!'

Pukka

cooked, ripe (Hindi, from '*pakka*')

The word '*pakka*', which means 'cooked' or 'ripe', is used in India to denote something that is first-class or completely authentic. The term entered the English language during the days of the Raj and is now generally used as slang for 'top quality'. It has been popularized in recent years by celebrity chef Jamie Oliver, who coined the phrase 'pukka tukka' to describe an expertly cooked dish.

'Come on, ladies and gents: salt and pepper pots, a pound a pair. That's a pukka pot of pepper, if ever I saw one.'

Pundit

learned man (Sanskrit)

When Britain began trading with India in the 1600s 'pundits', sometimes known as '*pandita*', were wise men who had studied Sanskrit history and traditions. They were revered as teachers and were important to the English traders in helping them to understand Indian customs. Over time, the word has come to be used for any expert or commentator who can explain events or developments in their area of expertise.

> *'For viewers unfamiliar with the rules of llama racing, our pundits at the race track will talk you through the basics.'*

Red Sammy, to win, in the 3.30 at Epsom.

❧◦❦◦❧

Purdah

curtain, veil (Hindi)

Originating in Persia in around 1000 BC, 'purdah' is a system of rules governing the movements and dress of women in some Hindu and Muslim societies. It requires women to cover themselves with a veil or burqa and to be separated from male non-family members by a curtain. In English we also use the word to mean any period of isolation, and in politics we use it to refer to the inactive period after the announcement of a general election or budget.

'Come on, Hannah – put this sparkly wig on and come for a drink, there's no point going into purdah just because you're having a bad hair day.'

⁓✦⁓

Pyjamas

trousers (Persian, from '*paijama*')

The original '*paijama*' are loose, lightweight trousers with drawstring waistbands worn in Asia by both sexes – literally '*pai*' meaning 'leg', and '*jama*' meaning garment. In the UK, pyjamas are loose-fitting, two-piece garments worn for sleeping, but sometimes also for lounging. For British children, pet abbreviations are popular and differ between families. These include 'jamas', 'p-jays' and 'jimmy jams'. Whatever word you're brought up with is correct and the other terms are weird.

If Molly could only get out of her pyjamas by midday it would be a big step towards getting a career.

⁓✦⁓

QED (Quod Erat Demonstrandum)

that which was to be demonstrated (Latin)

Ancient Greek mathematicians, including Archimedes and Euclid, used a similar phrase at the conclusion of a proven mathematical truth to indicate that they had worked out their solution ('that which' they had intended to show) using logical deductions. Mathematical books were written in Latin during the European Renaissance, when the phrase was adopted by philosophers to add weight to their arguments. We now use it at the end of any statement we deem to be irrefutable.

A diet low in red meat and high in fruit and vegetables is good for controlling obesity. You never see a fat vegetarian. QED.

---◦◦◦◦---

Quasi

as if (Latin)

In Latin this phrase was employed in exactly the same way that we would use the words 'as if', but over time it has come to be used as a prefix to words such as 'scientific', 'historical', 'official' and 'religious', to indicate that something is almost, or has some resemblance to the word it precedes. It provides us with a useful linguistic tool for describing things that can nearly, but not quite, be placed into a category we are familiar with.

> *'I want a new TV, not a science lesson, so skip the quasi-technological sales patter and tell me how much it costs.'*

---◦◦◦◦---

Que sera sera

whatever will be, will be (Portuguese/Spanish/French)

It's not actually clear which language this happy-go-lucky phrase comes from. It was the title of a 1956 song by Jay Livingston and Ray Evans which became a hit after Doris Day sang it for the Alfred Hitchcock film *The Man Who Knew Too Much*. Livingston said he'd adapted it from '*che sera sera*', a motto from the 1954 film *The Barefoot Contessa*, which may in turn have been taken from Christopher Marlowe's sixteenth-century play *Dr Faustus*.

> *Kay's attempt at seeming nonchalant about the promotion was rather spoiled by the volume at which she belted out 'Que Sera Sera' on her way to the interview.*

Quid pro quo

something for something (Latin)

In law this Latin term is used to describe an equal exchange, either to ensure good behaviour by requiring that services or goods are exchanged for something of equal value, or to prevent bad behaviour by ensuring, for example, that donors to political parties don't expect favours in return. We now also use it more generally to describe a situation that is mutually beneficial. The slang word 'quid' for 'pound sterling' is also derived from this phrase and its association with currency and exchange.

'An excellent meal, Charles, and it's my treat. No, really, I insist; quid pro quo – you've been a marvellous host all week.'

Raconteur

skilled storyteller (French)

This French word comes from the verb '*raconter*', meaning to relate or recount and is used to describe people with a sort of refined version of the 'gift of the gab'; in other words, someone known for their wit and skill at telling stories. It was first used in English in the nineteenth century, just in time for one of the world's most celebrated raconteurs, Oscar Wilde, to be labelled with the term.

Billy felt a bead of perspiration trickle down his neck as the first of his witty anecdotes was met with silence. He'd never been much of a raconteur and suddenly he understood that he just wasn't cut out to be best man.

Raison d'être

reason for being (French)

Originally used straightforwardly to rationally justify the existence of a thing, person or organization, the phrase has been used in English since 1864 to describe an individual's primary motivation in life, or dearest passion. If there is a cause that someone dedicates all their time to fighting for, or a project or hobby that they feel more passionate about than anything else, that might be described as their *raison d'être*.

Quentin came to life as he heard those rumba rhythms; dancing had been his raison d'être *since the day he first realized his hips knew how to wiggle.*

Rapport

harmonious relationship (French)

When this word was first used in English in the mid 1800s it was in the context of the psychologist–patient relationship. The earliest written record is Edgar Allen Poe's 1844 short story 'A Tale of the Rugged Mountains', in which Poe uses it to describe the magnetic bond between a practitioner of mesmerism (early hypnosis) and his subject. The word is still used in psychology, though we now also use the term to refer to any feeling of connection or emotional affinity between two people.

Lucy stood at the edge of the red carpet and quivered; Brad had only glanced at her for a second while he signed his autograph on her fake plastercast, but she was sure he too had felt the rapport *between them.*

Reductio ad absurdum

reduction to the absurd (Latin)

Another Latin term useful in both mathematics and philosophy, '*reductio ad absurdum*' is a process of logical reasoning in which a mathematician or debater might prove his or her own theorem to be correct by starting out with the opposite claim and showing that it leads to a ridiculous outcome. When their careful calculations demonstrate that it is wrong, they have succeeded in proving that their own claim is right.

'Birds are most certainly invertebrate animals that fly.'
'Are they? You don't think that the flightless emu and the ostrich furnish the reductio ad absurdam *for your proposition?'*

Renaissance

rebirth (French)

This is the name given to the period of radical cultural change that took place across Europe in the fifteenth and sixteenth centuries. The movement began in Italy where scholars called it the '*rinascita*' – the rebirth – in recognition of the fact that they had escaped the barbarism of the Middle Ages and were rediscovering the cultural values of Ancient Rome and Greece. The French translated the word and as England entered its own modern era we borrowed the French term. We now use it to describe any kind of revival.

Sandra carried her old clothes down from the attic with reverence. She was a shoulder-pad girl at heart and was thrilled that eighties fashions were having a renaissance.

Rickshaw

man-powered carriage (Japanese)

These two-wheeled carriages were originally pulled along by a runner and were first used in Japan in around 1868. The word is a shortened version of '*jinrikisha*' – a blend of three Japanese words, '*jin*', meaning 'man', '*riki*', meaning 'power', and '*sha*', meaning 'carriage'. It was popularized in English by Rudyard Kipling's 1888 ghost story 'The Phantom Rickshaw' and is now used to describe the bicycle-drawn carriages that clog the streets of Central London and downtown New York.

Jack had always agreed with Samuel Johnson that when a man is tired of London he is tired of life, but the day he was run over by a rickshaw he realized that Johnson's London was sadly not comparable with his own.

Lucky fellow, jolly good exercise.

———◦◦◦———

Rigor mortis

stiffness of death (Latin)

Ancient Roman physicians carrying out the earliest autopsies used this term to describe the rigidity of the body after death. Within three to six hours of death chemical changes in the muscles, combined with a build-up of lactic acid, cause the body to stiffen unless it is carefully cooled ready for embalming. The development of rigor mortis can be useful in determining the time of death in police investigations.

'I'm afraid Snowy's grave is going to have to run the full length of your rose garden, dear; it didn't occur to me that rabbits got rigor mortis.'

———◦◦◦———

Robot

drudgery (Czech)

The Czech word '*robota*' means 'drudgery', hence 'robot' for devices that can do tedious work for humans. The Czech writer Karel Čapek first introduced the concept, and name, of 'robot' in his play *R.U.R. (Rossum's Universal Robots)*, whose first scene takes place in a factory that manufactures artificial people to work for humans. There are many different definitions of what constitutes a modern robot, but broadly speaking they are programmable electro-mechanical systems that can sense and interact with their environment. In popular imagination, robots are machines with human qualities and capabilities, but whether they could ever possess true intelligence continues to intrigue philosophers, scientists, writers and film-makers alike.

Professor Zoton deliberately didn't give his robot, Epsilon-TransnegativeElectrostabilizer, a name in case he became too attached to him. Nevertheless it would have been easier to call him 'Pete'.

Roué

debauched or lecherous man (French)

This is a rare example of a name that is derived from the kind of punishment that ought to befall the person given it. The word is the past participle of '*rouer*', which means to break on a wheel or beat harshly, which the French felt was a fitting treatment for such a dissipated creature. These days, society is less critical of lechery and the word is often used for sex-hungry men who are regarded as 'players'.

> *'I'd steer clear of that Les Fisher if I were you, Jeanette. Apparently he's become a bit of a roué since he discovered Just For Men.'*

Rucksack

back bag (German)

What is often thought of as a peculiarly British word is actually borrowed from the Germans. It may have come into use during the era of Romanticism, which thrived in Germany and saw many an awe-inspired poet seeking the sublime on the kind of mountain walks that it would have been foolhardy to attempt without a rucksack of provisions. In Germany itself, the rucksack is often called a 'body bag', which doesn't sound quite so wholesome.

'For goodness' sake, Doreen, how do you expect me to find the compass when you insist on filling every crevice of the rucksack with egg and cress sandwiches?'

Safari

journey (Swahili)

In Swahili a 'safari' is any journey, even just nipping to the local market and back, but in English it is reserved for tours of the Savannah made especially to see and photograph the wildlife. It is thought to have been brought into the English language by explorer Sir Richard Francis Burton in the nineteenth century, when the phrase 'point and shoot' had rather different connotations. Hunting safaris are now rare and the term has extended to include wildlife-watching trips to rainforests, frozen tundra and remote parts of the ocean.

'We thought about going on a safari this year, didn't we, Jeff? But then we thought, well, we get a lot of quite sizeable cats in the garden at home, so we stuck with Camber Sands.'

Sangfroid

cold blood (French)

Though the literal translation makes the term sound vaguely reptilian, 'sangfroid' is – in both French and English – a desirable quality in a person. It arrived in English during the Enlightenment in the eighteenth century and means cool-headedness and composure. An important attribute in all reasoning individuals, sangfroid implies an ability to keep a clear mind and an even temper in the most testing of circumstances.

> *'Did you see her face as the nominations were read out? It was completely expressionless; I don't know whether to admire her sangfroid or blacklist whoever does her Botox.'*

Sarong

covering (Malay)

The sarong is the Malay national garment and the word was first recorded in 1834. It is made from a long sheet of fabric, often batik dyed, or woven with checks for men, which is tied at the waist. It is still worn by both men and women in South-East Asia, but in the West they are worn exclusively by women and David Beckham.

> *Toby waited for a good ten minutes after Sophie had left the house and then crept over to her wardrobe. He'd once been told he looked like David Beckham and he wanted to see if he could carry off a sarong.*

Savoir faire

know how to do (French)

In both French and English, this phrase refers to the kind of innate social knowledge possessed by tactful people who know instinctively how to behave, though the French version has more practical overtones and can refer to depth of knowledge in a particular field. The phrase was first recorded in English by Sir Walter Scott in his 1815 novel *Guy Mannering*, in which a character called Gilbert Glossin is described as having 'great confidence in his own *savoir faire*' when it came to his polished behaviour in society. Today we also use the informal shortened adjective 'savvy' for 'clued-up'.

'This isn't a job for Daniel – I know he tries hard, but he has as much savoir faire *as a baby chihuahua.'*

Schadenfreude

pleasure taken from another's suffering (German)

This comes from two German words, '*Schaden*', meaning damage or harm, and '*Freude*', meaning joy. Though it sounds like a mean and disturbed emotion to feel, *Schadenfreude* actually forms the basis of much of our comedy. From the slapstick antics of Charlie Chaplin to the self-deprecatory humour of modern stand-up comedians, as long as suffering isn't permanently damaging, it can be enjoyable to witness. The modern obsession with following the downfall of troubled celebrities is proof of the word's continuing usefulness.

Mary couldn't bear circus clowns, the Schadenfreude *the rest of the audience experienced from watching them fall over just left her with a nervous headache.*

Schlep
drag (Yiddish)

This comes from the Yiddish word '*shlepn*', meaning 'to drag or pull' and it has retained this meaning in one of its modern uses, in which it is synonymous with the English word 'lug'. It is more frequently used though to describe an arduous or difficult journey, and most recently, to describe any journey, however short or simple, that you simply can't be bothered to make.

'Oh, darling, please can we just get in a taxi, it's such a schlep to get to the West End and my Manolos don't deserve this kind of pounding.'

Schmaltz

rendered fat (Yiddish)

In brutally literal terms, 'schmaltz' is rendered pig, chicken or goose fat that is clarified and eaten spread onto bread, in the way that lard used to be before we knew about the dietary causes of heart disease. It arrived in English in the 1930s courtesy of Yiddish-speaking Jews who used it in this culinary sense, but it has been adapted by English speakers, along with the newly coined 'schmaltzy' to describe something excessively maudlin or 'dripping' with sentimentality.

'I know musical theatre is meant to be sentimental but the schmaltz levels in this one are just suffocating.'

Schmooze

converse casually (Yiddish)

This is one of those brilliant words that perfectly distils into a single syllable a fairly complex social interaction. It is believed to originate from the Hebrew word *'schmu'ot'*, which translates as 'reports' or 'gossip', and is used in Yiddish, and now English, to describe the act of exchanging small talk with someone in order to establish a mutually beneficial relationship with them. It's the 'chatting-up' of the business world.

Tara downed her glass of pinot grigio, applied a fresh coat of lipstick and spritzed on some perfume – she was ready to schmooze.

Schmuck/schmo

penis (Yiddish)

'Schmuck' and its slightly less offensive derivative 'schmo', have meanings synonymous with 'idiot', 'sad case' and the somewhat less refined 'dickhead'. Like the latter of these derogatory appellations, both come from the Yiddish word for penis and are used in English, primarily in America, as insults. The Yiddish 'schmuck' is linked to the same word in German, where it means 'jewels', which may or may not be the source of the popular euphemism 'the crown jewels'.

'Gregory, you've got to help me; some schmuck's just let his dog do its business on the wheel of my vintage Aston Martin.'

Shaman

priest (Russian/Evenki)

A religious practitioner serving the small, nomadic communities in Siberia, Mongolia and Northern China is known by the local Evenki-speaking people as a Shaman. Shamanism works on the principle that the lives of those on earth are shaped and influenced by spirits, over whom a Shaman has power. The word is now used in many different cultures to describe priest or sorcerers, and in the West the New Age community uses the term for its spiritual leaders.

'*Get those bits of half-chewed chicken bone off me, Steve! Thinking you saw a ghost on a short cut through the churchyard by the pub does not make you a shaman.*'

Sic

thus, in such a way (Latin)

Used in publishing to indicate a misspelling or unconventional use of a word, '*sic*', written in square brackets, is the editor's way of indicating that they are aware of the error but are simply quoting material in exactly the form in which it first appeared. It is especially useful for publications whose readership is proud of its pedantry and takes pleasure in writing in to point out syntactical oversights.

In a heartfelt letter to the Prime Minister, five-year-old Scarlet Jones wrote, 'I'm getting to like you more now, but I do miss Tony Bear [sic].'

Sine qua non

without which not (Latin)

This phrase, in its Greek form, was originally used by Aristotle to describe a legal condition that was absolutely essential and could not be done without. It has been used in English since around 1600 and the term is still used in this way in the British legal system, but has also been adopted more widely to mean any crucial ingredient or prerequisite without which the normal order of things could not proceed.

'Let me just call Gustav to ask for a recommendation. Really, darling, how could you think of cooking for yourself; these days a personal macrobiotic chef is the sine qua non *of the Hollywood elite.'*

Skol

cheers (Danish/Norwegian/Swedish)

Like all groups of marauding invaders, the Vikings liked a little tipple at the end of the working day. The word they used to accompany a toast was '*skol*', which has often been mistranslated as 'skull' because of the Vikings' mythical practice of drinking out of the skulls of their victims. In fact the word comes from the old Norse word '*skál*', meaning 'shell' or 'bowl'.

Martin woke up dressed in a tutu and tied to a lamp post. He tried to piece together the events that had led him there but all he could remember was shouting 'skol' before everything went dark.

Skal

Skull

Smorgasbord

sandwich table (Swedish)

In Sweden a '*smörgåsbord*' is a type of varied meal in which numerous dishes are arrayed on a table for guests to choose whichever items they like. It consists of both hot and cold dishes and traditionally includes smoked fish and meatballs. English speakers borrowed the word as an alternative to 'buffet', but its idiomatic meaning has since broadened and it is used to describe any situation in which a range of choices are presented.

'You are all in for a treat tonight, ladies and gentlemen; we've got a veritable smorgasbord of acts to tempt and bedazzle you.'

Spiel

a play or game (German)

Quite what playing has to do with long-winded speeches isn't clear but the German word 'spiel' has been absorbed into English to describe an extravagant address or argument that is generally delivered in order to convince the listener to believe in something, or buy it. It comes from the Middle High German *'spilon'*, meaning 'to revel', so perhaps giving a spiel was more fun in the Middle Ages than it is today . . .

'An hour and twenty minutes I was trapped at the front door this morning trying to fend off that salesman! I thought I knew about cleaning, but after his spiel I was an expert in all twenty-seven different kinds of dust.'

Spiritus mundi

soul, spirit of the world (Latin)

The concept of *'spiritus mundi'* has its roots in the philosophy of Plato, but the phrase itself was coined by fifteenth-century German astrologer and occult philosopher Agrippa von Nettesheim. He used it as a label for the spirit element that he believed permeated the whole world, and was the force behind alchemy and occult occurences. The psychologist Carl Jung elaborated on these ideas when he discussed the idea of a collective subconscious and the term is still used by astrologers and spiritualists today.

Runa closed her eyes and jangled her bangle-laden wrists; she was about to channel images from the spiritus mundi *and liked there to be an appropriately grandiose build-up.*

Status quo

state in which (Latin)

Shortened from a longer Latin phrase '*status quo ante bellum*', meaning 'the state in which things were before the war', this was used in Roman diplomacy to negotiate a return to the previous order of things before a conflict. The phrase is still used to describe an existing political situation – Ronald Reagan famously said, 'Status quo, you know, is Latin for "the mess we're in".' And we now use it for any abiding set of circumstances that are either under threat of change or need changing.

Norman liked the fact that he'd worked in the same office for thirty years. For him, maintaining the status quo was one of life's true pleasures.

Subpoena

under penalty (Latin)

A subpoena is an official written instruction to an individual to testify in, or bring evidence to, court, or face punishment. However, in their bid to be more accessible to those unfamiliar with Latin legal terms, civil courts in England and Wales have recently replaced the word with the phrase 'witness summons', which does explain rather neatly what the Latin word means. In America the word is often spelled 'subpena'.

'Oh no, I can't believe it – I've got a subpoena.'
'I'm so sorry, Frank – that's terrible. Is it contagious, do you think?'

Temet nosce

know thyself (Latin)

'*Temet nosce*', the Latin translation of the Greek phrase '*gnothi seauton*', which was engraved in the forecourt of the Temple of Apollo at Delphi, dates back to the fourth century. It translates as 'know yourself', and carries with it the idea that you must first understand yourself before you can understand others around you. Exactly which of the great Greek scholars came up with this profound aphorism is not clear; it may have been Socrates, or possibly Pythagoras, or one of four other sages. It has long been used in English by those of a philosophical bent and has been widely quoted since it was used by the character of the Oracle in the 1999 dystopian sci-fi film *The Matrix*.

Higgins was a terrible drunk – his school motto had been 'Temet nosce' and he'd taken it so much to heart that he regularly bored his companions to tears with his obsessive self-analysis.

Terra firma

solid ground (Latin)

This phrase was used in the labelling of maps in the seventeenth century in order to distinguish areas of dry land from the parts covered by seas or oceans. We also use 'terra' as the scientific name for our planet, and 'terra firma' more colloquially to describe being on solid ground rather than aboard a ship or in a plane.

'Well, Stephanie, I've loved every minute of our cruise but after last night's rough waters I have to admit I'm glad to be back on terra firma.'

Tête-à-tête
head-to-head (French)

Come on, lads, don't argue.

This phrase can be used in French and English to describe any intimate meeting between two people where the arrival of a third party would be considered an intrusion. It flourished in eighteenth-century tea rooms, where gossip was rife and whispered exchanges of confidences over a Bath bun were the best form of entertainment available. Sadly in modern usage it has been appropriated by pushy middle-managers who are prone to suggesting 'a quick tête-à-tête' as if they want a cosy chat, when they actually mean is 'an intimidating personal assessment'.

'Martin, have you got a moment? Let's have a little tête-à-tête over coffee in the chill-out zone.'

Thug
thief (Hindi/Marathi)

In Hindi and Marathi (the fourth most spoken Indian language) '*thag*' was the name given to a member of an Indian network of gangs who murdered and robbed travellers and often strangled their victims. They operated well into the nineteenth century, when they were driven out by the British, and by 1839 the term had come to mean 'ruffian or 'cut-throat'. These days we use 'thug' to describe someone hired by criminal groups to do their dirty work, as well as any brutishly violent male.

Beverley walked like a thug, swore like a thug, swung a base-ball bat like a thug and terrorized all the local businesses. And yet nothing could quite play down the fact that he had a woman's name.

Tour de force

feat of strength (French)

Not to be confused with the Tour de France, an annual long-distance bicycle race, this epic-sounding French expression denotes an achievement that has required great skill or endeavour to complete. In recent years it has been somewhat devalued in literary circles through over-use by critics, who employ it too often to describe a well-crafted novel, but it's still a valid term of praise for an outstanding sporting or artistic achievement.

'Well, Jim, we were expecting to see some good bowling from you, but that was a tour de force!'

Tout de suite

at once (French)

This phrase became common in English during the Great War, when many British soldiers spent time fighting in France. Like many French phrases adopted by the English, it was often misspelled and sometimes deliberately mispronounced. In 1917, an edition of satirical magazine *Punch* ran a cartoon featuring a Tommy saying to inquisitive French children: 'Nah, then, alley [go] toot sweet, an' the tooter the sweeter.'

Mrs Kendle watched in horror as the head of the marzipan bride- groom wobbled off the wedding cake. She could hear the guests outside and knew she must reverse the decapitation tout de suite.

Trek

a long journey (Afrikaans)

Trek entered English in the nineteenth century from South Africa, where the word was used by the Boers for a journey by ox wagon. The Groot Trek (1835 onwards) refers to the journey made by ten thousand Boers, who journeyed north and north-east from the Cape Colony to escape British colonial rule. The word is univer- sally familiar thanks to *Star Trek*, the hugely popular long-running sci-fi story created by Gene Roddenberry, whose ashes made perhaps the longest trek possible when they were sent into space aboard space shuttle *Columbia* in 1992.

It was quite a trek up the hillside and along the ridge, but Sally was determined to boldly go where no girl in kitten heels had gone before.

Tsar

emperor (Russian)

In Russia, Bulgaria and Serbia, 'tsar' has been the name for the sovereign since the fourteenth century. The word is a Russian adaptation of the Latin '*Caesar*' (also the root of the German

'*Kaiser*') and was used to describe all Russian Emperors until 1917. English speakers have in turn adopted the word to describe any politically powerful figure with jurisdiction over a certain problem area, such as drugs tsar or a terrorism tsar.

> *'OK, staff, I'd like to announce a new appointment this term; Mr Jacobson is going to take on the role of punctuality tsar, so eight-thirty arrivals at the latest from all of you, or you'll have him to answer to.'*

Tsunami

harbour wave (Japanese)

The literal meaning of this Japanese word comes from '*tsu*', 'harbour', and '*nami*', 'waves'. However the waves that the word describes are not confined to harbours, nor do they have anything to do with tides, but rather deep sea earthquakes. They were observed as early as 426 BC, when the Greek historian Thucydides correctly suggested that they might be caused by tremors under the ocean. Nearly two hundred Japanese tsunamis have been officially recorded, and the high incidence of the phenomenon in the oceans around Japan has resulted in the adoption of their word across many languages, including English. The Indian Ocean tsunami of 2004 was one of history's worst natural disasters, with hundreds of thousands of casualties.

'I've never really liked the sea. All the seaweed, and sharks, and tsunamis . . . no, a bath once a week has always been more than enough splashing about for me.'

Tycoon

great lord (Japanese)

Shoguns or generals in the Japanese army were given the title *'taikun'*, meaning 'great lord or prince', and when Matthew Perry, Commodore of the US Navy, compelled Japan to open trading with the West in 1854, he took the word back home with him. Abraham Lincoln's cabinet members used it as a nickname for the President, and it has since come to describe powerful and wealthy businessmen who have made their fortune from a particular industry, such as oil or shipping.

Mr Chakrabarti's ever-expanding chain of menswear shops had led some wags to dub him 'the shirt and tycoon'.

Übermensch

superman (German)

This word was coined by Friedrich Nietzsche in his 1883 work *Thus Spoke Zarathustra*, in which he described a more evolved version of humankind – a superhuman in comparison with which mankind as we know it would seem as under-developed as apes. The word is used in English primarily in a philosophical context, though '*über*' is often turned into a prefix as an alternative to 'extremely' in phrases like '*über* cool'.

> *'It would take ten people working flat out on that project to get it done inside a week and there are only three of us – what does he think we are – team* Übermensch?'

Ukulele
jumping flea (Hawaiian)

The Ukulele was a Portuguese instrument originally called a '*braghuina*', but when Portuguese immigrants arrived in Hawaii in the nineteenth century and played it in front of the locals the Hawaiians adopted it as their own. They rechristened it the 'jumping flea' in reference to the way in which the musician's fingers jump up and down the fret board. The 'uke' reached mainland USA in 1915 at the Panama Pacific International Exposition and has been a mainstay of American music ever since.

> *'The hot favourite at the Alabama Ukulele Play-offs stepped onto the stage with a swagger – they didn't call him "Fourteen-fingered Frankie" for nothing.'*

Utopia
no place (Greek)

In 1516 Sir Thomas More wrote a book about a fictional island on which the community functioned in perfect harmony: he called the eponymous island 'Utopia' from the Greek words '*ou*', 'not' (which sounds nearly the same as '*eu*', 'good') and '*topos*', 'place', and the word has been used ever since to describe a flawless society.

Over the centuries many people have chased the ideal of a utopia, sometimes with disastrous results. The word's antonym is 'dystopia' ('*dus*' being Greek for 'bad') and is a nightmarish imagined world, such as the one created by George Orwell in *1984*.

> *Sunshine, sangria, friendly neighbours and endless golf courses, the map might have told him it was Southern Spain but Mick felt he'd found utopia.*

Vade mecum

go with me (Latin)

In the Middle Ages physicians, astrologers, parsons and tradesmen often carried with them small manuals filled with useful references and calculation aids appropriate to their field of expertise. These were called 'vade mecums' or 'go-with-mes' because they were taken everywhere, often suspended on a string or ribbon from the belt. We still use the term for any handy object or booklet that is carried on the person, and more widely for specialist handbooks.

> *Alan patted his top pocket anxiously and felt his heart rate calm as his fingers touched on the hard cover of his angler's vade mecum; he'd never had a successful fishing trip without it.*

——⟡——

Vampire

a nocturnal reanimated corpse
(Hungarian/Bulgarian/Ukrainian)

In folk tales, 'vampires' revisited loved ones and caused mischief or deaths where they'd once lived. The etymology of the word is unclear but it possibly stems from a Kazan Tatar word for 'witch'. The ancient vampire was bloated and dark-countenanced, unlike the nineteenth-century reinvention, which is gaunt and pale. The term entered English in the eighteenth century, when vampire superstitions arrived from the Balkans and Eastern Europe. Our best-known fictional vampire is the eponymous villain of Bram Stoker's *Dracula* (1897), which was inspired by the legends surrounding fifteenth-century Wallachian Prince Vlad the Impaler.

Poised over the alabaster neck of his beautiful victim, the vampire sniffed the air. Had she been eating garlic?

——⟡——

Vendetta

blood feud (Italian)

Originating from the Latin word '*vindicta*', meaning 'revenge', the Italian term 'vendetta' is most associated with Corsica. There it was the name for a social code whereby if a serious wrong was committed against a member of a family, it could only be righted by the murder of the wrongdoer. The word has now come to be used to describe any kind of long-standing grudge.

'Hello, I'd like to book an appointment for a fake tan, please, with anyone but Jacqueline; she's had a vendetta against me since I asked if she'd been tangoed and I don't want her deliberately giving me streaks.'

— ❦ —

Verbatim

word for word (Latin)

This term made the transition into English through the printed word. The full phrase '*verbatim et literatim*', meaning 'word for word and letter for letter' was used to indicate that a piece of text had been copied precisely, with no alterations to the spelling, grammar or meaning. It is now most commonly used in spoken English to explain that something someone has said has been repeated exactly.

> '*You know John Lennon didn't really write "Imagine", don't you? In actual fact, I did. I read it out at a poetry recital in sixty-nine; he must have been there are copied it down verbatim.*'

— ❦ —

Verboten

forbidden (German)

Gott im Himmel, they are right ... nothing about tunnels!

VERBOTEN!

This word had been an unremarkable feature of the German language from the end of the Middle Ages until the autocratic policies of Wilhelm II and later the Nazis imbued it with sinister undertones. It became familiar to English speakers during World War II, when signs reading '*Juden verboten*' appeared everywhere from shop doors to park benches. We now use it in place of 'forbidden', usually when we want to imply an element of authoritarianism, or sometimes just tongue-in-cheek.

> *'Have you heard the latest from the new management? No talking between breaks – they'll have "Laughter verboten" flashing up on our screen-savers before we know it.'*

Verbum satis sapienti

a word is enough for the wise (Latin)

This saying is attributed to the Ancient Roman playwright Plautus. It means that just a few words of explanation are adequate to explain a situation or concept to someone who is wise. It is used in English as an alternative to the phrase 'enough said'.

> *'Understood, Bernard,* verbum satis sapienti *– it's half a tin of cat food in the morning and the other half at night. We'll get along just fine without him, won't we, Felix.'*

Via

by way of (Latin)

This is such a commonly used word in English that it seems strange to think of it as foreign, but we owe its usefulness to the Ancient Romans, who said in three letters what the English language needs three words for. It is almost synonymous with our word 'through' but it implies more strongly that a solution or destination has been arrived at by dint of a little detour.

In a violent rage Jim ripped the satellite navigation system from the dashboard and threw it out of the car window. He'd reached the queue for the ferry before he realized that it was directing him from London to Birmingham via Calais.

⚬⚭⚬

Vice versa

a switched change (Latin)

The term is used to mean that the reverse of the previous statement, with the main items transposed, is also true. It is usually used to imply the complement of a statement without expressing as much in words. For example: 'Fish can't live where we are most comfortable, and vice versa'. It is usually pronounced as spelled, but in fact the correct pronunciation is 'wee-ce wer-sah'. The first English usage is found in print as early as 1601. A similar term, 'arsy versy', has now become archaic (and also sounds a bit rude).

Wives may bring their husbands to the celebration and vice versa (husbands may bring their wives).

⚬⚭⚬

Vis-à-vis

face-to-face (French)

This French expression was first used in English in the 1750s with a trio of different meanings. The name given to a carriage in which the passengers sat facing each other with their knees almost touching; a term used to describe a person or object opposite you;

and an alternative to 'in relation to'. The last of these is how we most commonly use the term today, with the idea that it's a more stylish substitute for 'regarding'.

> *'Hi, Katie! I, um, I wondered if I could talk to you vis-à-vis what happened, erm, you know, the other night. It's just that I'd had a few drinks and I didn't know if you, you know. So, ah, anyway, give me a call. If you want to. Obviously.'*

⸙

Voilà

see there (French)

This exuberant exclamation comes from the French word '*voir*', meaning 'to see', combined with '*là*', meaning 'there'. It's used in France and in English-speaking countries when some sort of action has been demonstrated successfully, and is particularly popular with television chefs, who often deliver it with a smack of the lips as they take a perfect pie out of the oven. The closest equivalent in English is 'there you have it', which doesn't have quite the same triumphant ring to it.

'Simply throw the chicken into a bowl with the turmeric and bean sprouts, pop it in the oven for thirty minutes and voilà*!'*

———◦◦◦———

Vox populi

voice of the people (Latin)

This is a reduced version of '*Vox populi, vox dei*', meaning 'the voice of the people is the voice of God', a phrase believed to date back to the eighth century that referred to a belief that the views of the masses should rule the day. Shortened to 'vox populi', it has come to mean 'the view of the majority', or a belief shared by most people. It is often shortened further to 'vox pop', which is now used in broadcasting to describe interviews with members of the public giving their views on a subject.

'Of course, if it were up to the people around this table we could all hunt as many bally foxes as we liked, Donald, but the vox populi says it's cruel, so we're stuck with clay pigeons I'm afraid.'

———◦◦◦———

Wanderlust

desire to travel (German)

This is a blend of German words '*wandern*', meaning 'to hike', and '*Lust*', meaning 'desire'. It was first used in English in the late nineteenth century; possibly as a result of our association of German Romanticism with carefree wandering. We still use it to refer to a yearning for the open road.

Pete had always planned to settle down by the time he was thirty, but wanderlust kept gripping him by the throat and dragging him back to mosquito-ridden swamps in far-flung places.

Wunderkind

wonder child (German)

In nineteenth-century Germany this phrase often referred to musical child prodigies such as Mozart and Beethoven, but the phrase has expanded to include anyone at an early age with a specific skill, art or talent. A ten-year-old with expert skills in, say, mathematics, chess or art deserves the title. In English the term has come to include those with remarkable talent or ability who achieve great success or acclaim early in their adult life. The computer industry has plenty of modern examples.

Troy may be the new wunderkind of alternative theatre but his mum still has to do his laundry.

Yin and yang

balance of opposites (Chinese)

In Chinese, '*yin*' denotes negative, dark, calm and feminine qualities, '*yang*' positive, bright, fiery, masculine ones. In Chinese philosophy, the concept of yin and yang describes how seemingly opposing forces are interconnected and interdependent in the natural world, giving rise to each other in turn. This idea lies at the heart of classical Chinese science and philosophy, and is a fundamental principle in traditional Chinese medicine. Many natural dualities – e.g. dark and light, female and male, low and high – are cast in Chinese thought in this way, and represented by the symbol '☯'.

> *'Yin and yang is a dynamic equilibrium,' said Huaqing sagely. 'Because they arise together they are always equal: if one disappears, the other must disappear as well, leaving emptiness.'*

Zeitgeist

spirit of the time (German)

The word describes the atmosphere of an era but can also refer to a trend. Literally translated: '*Zeit*' is time; '*Geist*' spirit. In German, the word has more layers of meaning than in English, including the fact that zeitgeist can only be observed for past events. The English usage is looser and the word carries a compelling literary ring, for anything that seems to perfectly capture a mood or a trend.

> *Lots of students in the sixties got caught up in street protest; the zeitgeist of the age compelled it. At least that was Tarquin's excuse when he became a judge.*

Brief list of sources

A New Dictionary of Eponyms, by Morton S. Freeman, Oxford University Press, 1998

Chambers Dictionary of Etymology, edited by Robert K. Barnhart, Chambers Harrap, 1999

Faux Pas? by Philip Gooden, A&C Black, 2007

Oxford Dictionary of English Etymology, edited by C. T. Onions, Oxford University Press, 1966

http://french.about.com
http://germanenglishwords.com
http://hinduism.about.com
http://latin-phrases.co.uk
www.absoluteastronomy.com
www.answers.com
www.bhashaindia.com
www.encyclopedia.com
www.muslimheritage.com
www.phrases.org.uk
www.thefreedictionary.com
www.uklegal.com
www.urbandictionary.com
www.websters-online-dictionary.org
www.word-detective.com
www.yourdictionary.com